SUCCESS WITH
SEEDS

SUCCESS WITH
SEEDS

Chris & Valerie Wheeler

GUILD OF MASTER CRAFTSMAN
PUBLICATIONS LTD

First published 2003 by
Guild of Master Craftsman Publications Ltd,
166 High Street, Lewes,
East Sussex, BN7 1XN

ISBN 1 86108 299 1

British Cataloguing in Publication Data
A catalogue record of this book is available from the British Library.

Edited by Graham Clarke
Designed by Andy Harrison
Front cover photograph by Anthony Bailey
Typeface: Futura

Colour origination by Universal Graphics Pte Ltd., Singapore

Printed and bound by Kyodo Printing Pte Ltd., Singapore

This book is dedicated to
the memory of Jem, Misty and Heidi

Contents

Introduction

Growing your own plants from seed is a very satisfying and exciting part of gardening. So many plants, ranging from annuals through bulbs to trees and shrubs, can be raised from seed successfully, either by collecting it yourself, or by purchasing commercial packets of seed.

Understanding what seeds are and the conditions under which successful germination is likely to occur is vital in order to propagate plants by seed.

This practical book is for gardeners of all abilities who are keen to try their hand at growing their own plants from seed.

Both popular and more unusual or challenging plants are included. The beginner can gain confidence whilst growing the easier plants, or by using the more basic techniques. Meanwhile, the more experienced gardener can experiment, and raise a wider range of plants.

This book is split into two sections. The first part discusses the nature of seeds and sources for obtaining them, and describes the skills and techniques required for germinating seeds and raising new plants.

The second part applies all this knowledge to specific groups of plants, with extra information and tips where necessary.

Few things in gardening are more satisfying than raising plants, perhaps some you have never grown before, right through from sowing a seed to achieving a fully mature plant.

LEFT Understanding the conditions for successful germination is the key to raising new plants from seed

SECTION 1

CHAPTER 1

What are seeds?

A seed contains the beginnings of a new plant. It is a living organism, with the embryonic plant encased in a protective coating. While in its resting, dormant state, metabolism continues at a very low rate, until it is stimulated by certain factors that start the growth process.

RIGHT **Leaves from two seed-raised acers, showing the variation in colour that can arise**

THE FUNCTION OF SEEDS

REPRODUCTION

Seed is the most common method by which plants naturally reproduce. Plants survive by reproducing themselves, again and again, ensuring that a new generation follows the current one. Successful reproduction is the key to survival for any plant in the wild, and it can be risky.

The next generation of plants need to establish themselves separately from the parent

ABOVE **Ripened seeds of a hellebore**

plant. Also, vast numbers of seeds (particularly if they are short-lived) may need to be produced to ensure that just a few will survive and grow to eventually produce their own seeds. Some seeds remain viable for years. Their resistance to drought and extreme temperatures enables them to survive long periods in adverse conditions, finally to germinate when conditions are right.

VARIATION

Reproduction by seed results in diversity among plant populations. Genes carried by pollen and ovules are combined together in different ways, creating new, individual plants. The transmission of a particular combination of genes makes up the

ABOVE **Seedhead of chives, showing some immature capsules and some ready to shed ripe seed**

unique characteristics of any given plant or group of plants – both its genetic make-up and what it looks like outwardly. Seed reproduction creates new individuals from a combination of the genetic make-up of the two parents, and the characteristics of the new plant will reflect this. A seedling will have traits or qualities of one or both parents, but will not be an exact replica of either.

Variation among plants is a consequence of this sexual reproduction, and over time enables plants to adapt to their environment. It also provides the basis for the breeding and selection of plants with new or more desirable traits or characteristics. Seeds may breed more or less true, but the variation within a plant species can be considerable.

5

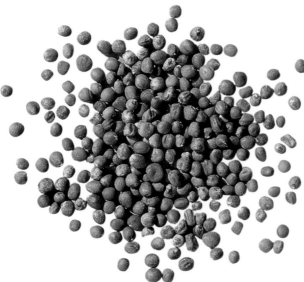

ABOVE **Seed of cabbage 'January King'**

ENERGY STORE

A seed must accumulate sufficient storage materials to support the initial growth of the seedling from the embryo. This mostly occurs towards the end of seed growth.

Carbohydrates are translocated (the process of moving water and nutrients around the vascular system of the plant) from the leaves of the plant, where they are produced by photosynthesis, to the seeds, where they are converted to more complex storage products in the form of carbohydrates, fats and proteins.

The successful accumulation of food reserves results in plumper, heavier seeds that will germinate well and produce vigorous seedlings that have a better chance of survival.

If insufficient storage material is collected, due to adverse conditions of any sort, seeds are more likely to be thin, shrivelled and light, resulting in poorer storage survival, less chance of germination and weaker seedlings. Minuscule amounts of the energy store within the seed are utilized even during its dormant or resting state, as the embryo is alive and requires nourishment. Much more is mobilized once germination begins, so it is vital that the seed has sufficient energy reserves.

In gardening terms, this means maintaining strong healthy plants if you are hoping to collect your own seed. Don't allow plants to dry out in the vital stages of seed maturing; make sure they have sufficient nutrients and keep pests and diseases at bay. Commercially produced seed undergoes stringent testing, and storage conditions are optimized, to ensure high quality seed.

TYPES OF SEED
SEED STRUCTURE

The seed is a matured ovule within the ovary or fruit. A seed consists of the embryo, the food storage tissues and the seed coverings. Seeds and fruits vary considerably in their shape, size and appearance between different plant species.

The embryo, produced by pollination and fertilization, is the potential new plant. One end grows into the shoot, the other into the root. Its shoot has one or more cotyledons (seed-leaves) attached. Flowering plants are classified according to the number of cotyledons. For example, monocotyledons (grasses, onions, hostas, etc.) have a single seed-leaf, while dicotyledons (the majority of flowering plants) have two. Gymnosperms (such as pine) may have several cotyledons.

Nourishing storage tissues surround the embryo, and around these is the seed-coat, which protects the embryo. There may be an inner and outer seed-coat. The inner coat is thin, transparent and membranous, while the outer coat changes during development. It often turns dry and hard, thickening and perhaps colouring, to produce the characteristic seed of a plant species. The hard seed-coat not only protects the embryo, but prevents further development of the new plant until suitable conditions arise (for example, water to soften the seed-coat).

DIFFERENT SEED SHAPES

ABOVE Lettuce 'Little Gem'

ABOVE RIGHT *Ipomoea*
'Heavenly Blue'
(morning glory)

RIGHT Cucumber 'Marketmore'

BELOW *Campsis radicans*

BELOW RIGHT
Eccremocarpus scaber

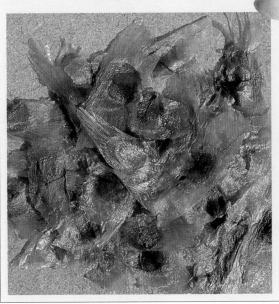

ABOVE *Erigeron* seeds have hairs attached to facilitate wind dispersal

SEED DISPERSAL

There are many ingenious ways in which plants disperse their seeds. The aim of seed production is to ensure survival, therefore seeds need to be dispersed preferably some distance from the parent plant.

The following methods are the main ways in which plants distribute their seeds.

Wind: Wind dispersal is achieved by several different methods.

● Seed can be so light that it is freely blown away by the wind.

● The seed pod may open in such a way that only a few seeds at a time are released, jerking out when the pod moves in the wind (for example, poppy, monkshood and iris).

● Flattened seeds are more easily dispersed by wind (for example, wallflower).

● Special structures attached to seeds enable them to be carried easily, such as the winged fruit of ash and birch, and the 'keys' of sycamore. Hairy attachments, or plumes, are found on the seeds or fruits of willow, *Epilobium*, *Clematis* and *Pulsatilla*. Many of the composites (daisy family) have hairs attached to the seeds, and here they are known as the pappus.

● Some seeds have the ability to roll in the wind.

There is always a greater loss of seed among wind-dispersed seeds, as they may land literally anywhere. Therefore plants with these types of seeds tend to produce them in more copious quantities than plants which utilize other dispersal methods.

Explosive mechanisms:
Seed can be flung out suddenly by the fruits actively moving, either by some part being swollen and stretched or by tensions caused by the drying of the fruit wall. This is particularly noticeable in plants in the genus *Geranium*, where the styles curl upwards and outwards, throwing out the seeds. In lupin and broom, the pods twist

ABOVE **Pods of *Lathyrus niger* open by twisting and thereby flinging out the seeds**

and separate, consequently flinging out the seeds.

Birds and animals: The fur of mammals can carry fruits with spines or hooks (for example, *Acaena*). The animal brushes against a plant, the hooked fruit attaches itself to the fur and becomes detached elsewhere. Birds and rodents consume fruits of various sorts, but the seeds themselves pass through the digestive system unharmed and are deposited elsewhere. In addition, there is the movement of seeds on the feet of animals and birds (and, of course, of man).

LEFT ***Anemone* seeds are light and fluffy, ideal for wind dispersal**

9

ABOVE **Each seed on this** *Pulsatilla* **head has a plume attached**

Water: Seed falling onto the surface of moving water may float away and be carried great distances. Plants with mechanisms for specific dispersal by water tend to be those growing in or near water.

WHERE SEEDS ARE FOUND ON PLANTS

We have already noted that the seed contains the embryo and food storage tissues, and develops after fertilization of the ovule. This is contained within the fruit, which develops from the ovary and sometimes other parts of the flower. The ovary wall becomes the fruit wall (pericarp), which may stay soft and fleshy or may dry out and harden.

Seeds and fruits develop and mature in different ways and take on various appearances in different plant species. Sometimes, seeds cannot be separated from the fruit as they become fused, or joined, into a single unit.

In these cases, the fruit is treated as the 'seed'. In some plants, parts of the fruit remain attached to the seed; again, the whole structure is treated as the 'seed'.

EXAMPLES OF FRUITS

Capsules are usually dry, many-seeded fruits that split naturally, allowing seeds to escape. In poppy (*Papaver*), the seeds are released through holes at the top of the rounded capsule; in pinks (*Dianthus*), the capsule splits halfway down to release the seeds; in willowherb (*Epilobium*), it splits longitudinally.

The fruits borne by peas and other legumes (and by *Laburnum*, for instance) are pods, which split along both sides when mature in order to release the seeds.

Achenial fruits are dry and one-seeded, and do not open naturally. Instead, the germinating embryo eventually ruptures both the seed-coat and the fruit wall. Members of the buttercup family have fruits consisting of a collection of achenes, and in *Clematis*, the head of achenes appears fluffy due to the persistent hairy styles.

ABOVE **Seeds of poppy escape through holes in the capsule**

Other types include daisy, sunflower (and other members of the Compositae family), and thistles. Each seed of these is attached to a fluffy structure known as a pappus, which facilitates wind dispersal.

Winged fruits of ash and elm are also achenial, as are nuts, in which the fruit wall is hard and woody (for example, hazel, beech and oak). Nuts are often enclosed in cupules, formed from structures at the base of the flower, such as the husk of hazelnut and cup of acorn.

Schizocarpic fruits are dry and many-seeded, splitting up as they dry into one-seeded parts. Many umbellifers, some legumes and crucifers (for example, radish), labiates and geraniums fall into this category.

Drupes are 'stone' fruits, consisting of an outer skin, a fleshy middle area, and the hard 'stone' that encloses the seed, usually single. Cherry and plum are examples. Compound drupes are also found, such as the 'berries' of holly and dogwood. Blackberries and raspberries are collections of simple drupes.

True berries are composed of a succulent pulpy mass with the hard seeds embedded in it. Currant, cucumber, grape and orange are examples. The date is a berry, as the 'stone' is the seed itself, not just the hard outer covering protecting the seed within.

In the rose family (Rosaceae) the receptacle – the part above the flower stalk – often enlarges, becoming the prominent part of the fruit. For example, in the genus *Malus*, the receptacle forms the fleshy part – the apple – with the familiar apple pips (the seeds) in the centre. In the case of the strawberry, the fleshy receptacle bears numerous seeds all around the outside.

POLLINATION

Most flowering plants are hermaphrodite, each flower bearing both male and female parts. The male parts are the stamens, made up of the filament and anther (which bears the pollen). The female part is the ovary with a style and one or more stigmas. As the flower matures, pollen from the stamens is transferred onto the stigmas. If these are on the same flower, it is known as 'self-pollination'. If they are on a different flower of the same species (whether the same or another plant), it is 'cross-pollination'. Pollen can be transferred in several ways: by insects, birds, wind or water. In some species it is

highly specialized so that only one particular insect can pollinate that plant.

The pollen, after it has been transferred from anther to stigma, grows down the style until it reaches the embryo sac, where fertilization occurs between the pollen and a ripe ovule. The embryo, with its potential for a new plant, develops from this.

The petals of a flower can attract pollinators, as can nectar and perfume. Many plants have mechanisms in their flowers that encourage cross-pollination rather than self-pollination. These usually favour cross-pollination while leaving open the possibility of self-pollination.

However, sometimes self-pollination is impossible or very difficult. Some flowers are unisexual, bearing only stamens or only the female parts, in which case cross-pollination is the only option.

A plant that is monoecious bears both male and female flowers on the same plant, so cross-pollination between flowers on the same or different plants is possible. However, dioecious plants, such as willow (*Salix*), bear male and female flowers on different plants, so cross-pollination must be between different plants and is therefore more difficult.

It is usually recommended for male and female varieties of certain plants – mainly trees and shrubs – to be grown in close proximity in order to have the maximum potential for fruiting or berry production (for example hollies, skimmia, etc.).

Some plants are self-sterile, meaning the flower cannot be pollinated by its own pollen, only by pollen from a different flower. In other cases, anthers

LEFT A split capsule of *Dianthus*

RIGHT Runner bean pods, which shed seeds by splitting down both sides

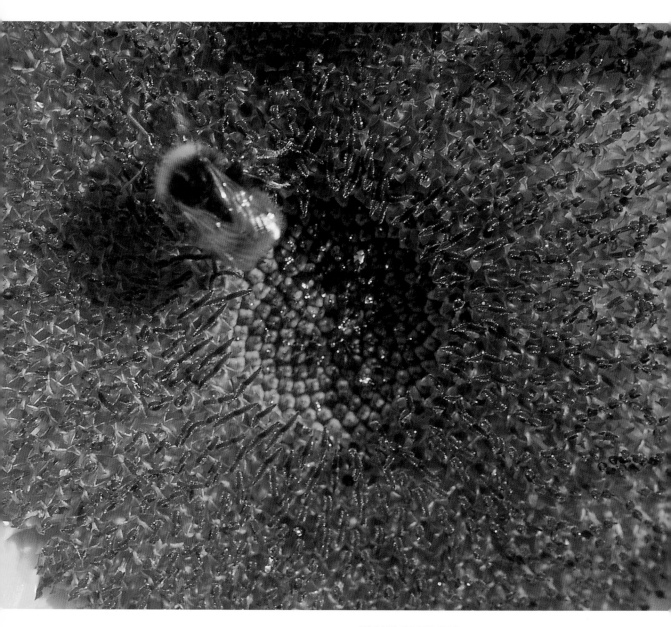

ABOVE **Pollen being picked up by a bee**

and stigma may mature at different times, making self-pollination less likely.

It is important to understand the various forms of pollination if you start to collect and raise your own seed, and particularly if you want to cross certain plants to produce seed.

PLANT BREEDING
WHY BREED PLANTS?

Many cultivated plants little resemble the wild species from which they were developed. The changes wrought in so many of our garden and food plants are the results of selection by man. Modern breeding programmes are often scientific and deliberate, selecting specific traits to produce larger or brighter flowers, more

14

paper bag. Previously collected pollen of the desired male parent is transferred to the stigma when it is receptive. The flower is then further protected against insects until fertilization has taken place. The resulting hybrid seed develops and is collected when ripe.

A hybrid is the offspring of two individuals that differ from each other in one or more characters. Seed saved from hybrids does not 'come true'. In other words, it will not be identical to the hybrid parent, and may revert to one or more of the genetic characteristics from its ancestry.

A breeder is looking for many different but desirable qualities in new plants: these include the size, colour, form and quantity of flowers, or a high-yielding fruitfulness (particularly of crops and vegetables), and plant vigour or form. Roses and dahlias, for instance, have been bred in a vast range of flower shapes and colours.

F1 AND F2 HYBRIDS

Seeds of F1 and F2 hybrids are produced by a complex technique of plant breeding, resulting in plants that are as nearly perfect and uniform as they can be. They are invariably more expensive than open-pollinated seed, and tend to be limited to annuals (bedding plants), vegetables and crops.

An F1 hybrid is the result of hand-pollination between two parent plants. It is the 'first filial generation', produced by crossing two genetically inbred plants of the same species. Greater uniformity occurs with inbreeding, and at the same time more vigour results from the cross-breeding, allowing both benefits. The same cross must be repeated every time the seeds are produced.

Many flowering annual and summer bedding plants offered by seed firms are F1 hybrids. They have been bred for earlier, more prolific or longer flowering, and some have had the ability to flower in duller or cooler weather bred into them. Others have been bred to produce more

even crops, greater disease resistance or hardiness, and so on.

OUTLINE OF METHOD USED

In hybridizing plants, self-pollination needs to be avoided. To ensure cross-pollination, the breeder removes the male parts from the designated female parent, and then protects the flower by enclosing – or preferably sealing – it in a

ABOVE **A hellebore flower showing immature anthers surrounding central stigmas**

uniform plants in colour and size (particularly important for container-growing and bedding), for new or improved flower colour, and to produce more vigorous plants.

Seed firms also offer F1 vegetables. These may have more resistance to disease, be earlier cropping, higher yielding, have better flavour, or have more weather resistance (for example, more frost-tolerant winter cabbages). F1 hybrid vegetables have even been bred for different colours, such as yellow carrots (in the case of 'Yellowstone F1 Hybrid'). Some courgette F1 hybrids produce largely female flowers, ensuring heavier yields.

An F2 hybrid, or 'second filial generation', occurs when four selected lines are used for two controlled crosses. In other words, F2 hybrids are the immediate descendants from self-pollinated or inter-pollinated F1 plants. This retains some of the vigour and uniformity of the F1 parents, but allows other characteristics to show through as well. Some annuals are commonly available as F2 hybrids, notably geraniums (pelargoniums) and pansies.

GERMINATION

Germination is the process in which the seed becomes a young plant, and involves all the changes that occur during this process. There are several stages in seed germination.

GERMINATION PROCESS

A seed separated from the parent plant, although dry and appearing to be dormant, is in fact at a very low level of activity. During germination, the metabolism of the cells increases rapidly and visible activity occurs.

Assuming the seed is viable (that is, alive and capable of germinating) and the conditions are favourable, germination takes place in the following stages:

1. The seed absorbs water, increasing the

moisture content and causing the seed to swell. This may also cause the seed-coat to rupture.

2. Metabolism increases, particularly respiration, so the seed requires oxygen. It must not, therefore, be waterlogged.

3. The embryo grows as a result of the food material stored in the seed being broken down and moved into the growing points.

4. New tissues are consequently formed, resulting in growth of the embryo. The embryo consists of an axis with the growing point of the root (radicle) at one end and the growing point of the shoot (plumule) at the other, and also bears the seed-leaves (cotyledons). The radicle elongates and grows downwards to form the root while the plumule develops into the shoot.

TYPES OF GERMINATION

The appearance of the young seedling may vary depending on the type of germination, whether epigeal or hypogeal.

In epigeal germination, the cotyledons emerge above the soil, turning green, enlarging and becoming the first leaves. The plumule, or growing shoot, is concealed between the cotyledons and, as they open out, it develops and grows into the shoot, bearing the true leaves of the plant. This is why the first pair of leaves of many seedling plants appears different to those that follow: the first is a simple pair of leaves (the cotyledons) while the rest are the true leaves. Examples include sunflower and cherry.

In hypogeal germination, the cotyledons remain below ground and the plumule emerges from the soil, at first arched over and then straightening out. The first leaves formed may be simpler than later ones, but they are still true leaves. Examples include broad bean and peach.

In monocotyledons (such as grasses, pine and daylily), the embryo has only one cotyledon, which usually remains below ground. The radicle develops strongly at germination but is then replaced by other roots developing from the base of the stem, forming a fibrous root system.

ABOVE **A developing seedling clearly showing the new root (radicle) and shoot (plumule)**

OVERCOMING DELAYED GERMINATION

Most seeds cannot germinate while within the fruit attached to the parent plant, or even for a time after the fruit has ripened and the seed has been dispersed.

Quiescent, or non-dormant, seed is able to germinate immediately, as long as favourable environmental conditions are provided. Dormant seed, on the other hand, is prevented from germinating by its own external or internal mechanisms. These may be present for a variety of reasons:

ABOVE **In hypogeal germination, the new shoot emerges arched over to protect the tip – the cotyledons remain below ground**

● To control the onset of germination in order to coincide with favourable environmental conditions, thereby giving the seedling a better chance of survival.

● The seed-coat may be hard and impermeable, requiring some injury in order to absorb water.

● The embryo may be immature when seed is first shed, so it continues growing within the seed and does not germinate until mature enough.

● Seed-coats may contain chemical inhibitors, which need to be reduced by leaching.

● Seed may need further ripening even though the embryo is fully developed. This type of dormancy can be regulated by the seed covering, or by conditions within the embryo, or by both.

Depending on the cause of seed dormancy, the gardener or grower can overcome this by various means. These include soaking seeds in water just prior to sowing, nicking the hard seed-coating to allow water absorption,

moist-chilling (stratification) for a short or prolonged period, or by providing alternate warm and cold, moist periods.

Some conifers and other woody plants produce seeds whose dormancy can be overcome by moist-chilling. This is not essential, but does speed up the process. The horticultural term is stratification, and involves placing seeds in layers of moist sand or soil and exposing them to chilling temperatures (outdoors over winter or in refrigerated conditions).

A more prolonged cold period can eliminate the dormancy found in seeds of many trees and shrubs and some herbaceous plants. These plants normally shed their seed in autumn, where it overwinters in the ground and germinates in more favourable conditions in spring. This is a common type of dormancy for the woody plants of temperate and colder climates.

Within this group, some seeds require a warm period followed by a cold, moist period (some lilies, and peony, for example). Others require a cold period followed by a warm period, followed by another cold period.

In cases where double dormancy occurs (in various trees and shrubs), both the seed-coat and the embryo dormancy need to be broken in sequence, so required treatments need to be given in sequence. This is a challenge for growers as the pre-germination period can be up to two years.

FACTORS AFFECTING GERMINATION

The key factors affecting germination are water, temperature and light.

Water: Affecting both the percentage and the rate of germination, water availability is crucial. The gardener needs to maintain a uniform moisture supply whilst at the same time providing adequate drainage. Seeds need to be sown in well-aerated seed compost or soil and watered frequently. If the seeds dry out germination will be delayed and reduced. Waterlogging will cause less oxygen to be available to the developing seedlings, and can also encourage 'damping off'.

Seeds can be soaked prior to planting, which can shorten the germination time, but more care is needed when sowing as the seeds are more liable to injury. Be careful not to soak the seed for too long, which can be harmful, reducing the amount of oxygen available to the seed.

Temperature: In nature, temperature frequently determines the time of year germination occurs. Therefore, the gardener may need to regulate the temperature to achieve germination when wanted. Many seeds have minimum and maximum temperatures at which they will germinate. Some seed may indeed germinate at a low temperature, but the germination success rate increases the warmer the temperature, up to an optimum level. You will find that seed of many cultivated plants, which go through seed-handling operations and a period of dry storage, germinate over a wide temperature range.

'High temperature sensitivity' is found in many vegetable crops, which require low temperatures, and fail to germinate in temperatures higher than, say, 25°C (77°F). Lettuce and celery are well-known examples. In nature this would prevent germination after seed dispersal in hot, dry summers.

Light: This can stimulate or inhibit the germination of some seeds. Light-requiring seeds include lettuce, celery, most grasses, many herbaceous plants and many conifers. Light requirement can disappear with dry storage, or can be overcome by various treatments.

ABOVE **Runner bean seeds germinate more rapidly if soaked in water first**

ABOVE **After a few hours of being soaked, the seeds have swollen considerably**

CHAPTER 2

Sources of seed

Seeds are available from a number of sources, primarily from retail or mail-order outlets, specialist plant societies or by collecting your own seeds from garden plants. Some gardeners and plant specialists enjoy going on seed collecting expeditions, either close to home or in far-off foreign parts.

BUYING SEEDS
RETAIL OUTLETS

Most garden centres stock a wide range of seeds, while a smaller selection is usually available from local hardware and garden shops. Supermarkets often stock a limited range comprising the more popular varieties.

ABOVE *Heteropappus saxomarinus,* grown from seed purchased from a Russian seed collector found via the internet

ABOVE *Lilium formosanum* var. *pricei* is an easy bulb to grow from your own collected seed

ABOVE We have donated seed of the unusual *Armeria euscadensis* to exchange schemes

ABOVE **A seed collecting expedition to New Zealand was the source for this unusual dwarf sedge,** *Luzula pumila*

Seeds bought from retail outlets are usually enclosed in pictorial packets that include detailed growing instructions, making them ideal for those new to sowing seeds. Seed packets are usually stamped on the back with a date. This shows either that they were packed in a certain year or that they should be sown by the end of a particular year. Seeds that were not packed during the previous year, or that have passed their sow-by date should be rejected, as they are likely to be poor germinators. Particular care should be taken when buying from smaller outlets that may have a slow turnover of stock.

Many seed firms indicate on the packets that the seeds are ideal for beginners. The varieties in these ranges may be very common, but they are an ideal starting point if you are new to propagation. If you follow the instructions on the packets then you should begin to see some results very quickly.

MAIL ORDER

Mail-order seed catalogues offer the widest choice of seeds. Several companies also supply garden centres and shops, but with only a small proportion of their range. Their catalogues are lavishly illustrated with many tempting and exciting varieties. Smaller companies tend to offer a more specialized range, concentrating in some cases on just one genus or perhaps just rare and unusual plants.

Some of these catalogues provide very detailed growing instructions while others are just a list of plant names aimed at enthusiasts with their own sources of information.

There is a great deal of variation between firms in the way they classify their seed. Some of the common terms and abbreviations are listed below:

HA	Hardy annual
HHA	Half-hardy annual
HB	Hardy biennial
HP	Hardy perennial
HHP	Half-hardy perennial
HHP	treat as HHA Usually used to describe perennial plants that may be tender or naturally short-lived and are therefore best grown as annuals each year
TP	Tender perennial
IP	Indoor plant /Houseplant

One of the biggest differences between seed companies is the amount of seed that you get in each packet. There is no common standard to describe this, though the following information is often given:

● Weight of seed
● Number of seeds
● Enough seed for x plants

The weight of seed is of no use unless you know how many seeds there are in each gram. The number of seeds is a better guide but the number of plants you will get depends on the germination percentage of the seeds. Enough seed for x plants is the best description as it takes all the variables into account.

The amount of seed within each packet depends on several different things.

● How much seed the plant produces – if a variety only produces a small amount of seed each year then the amount in each packet will be much smaller than that of a variety that produces a mass of seed.
● The size of the seeds – physically large seeds tend to be sold in smaller quantities, simply to fit the seed into the packet.

● The cost of producing the seed – F1 hybrid seed, in particular, is expensive to produce and this is reflected in the price, which may seem high for the quantity of seed received.
● Individual companies – there are considerable variations in the number of seeds of the same variety in packets sold by different companies. It pays to shop around, particularly for expensive varieties.

Browsing through mail-order seed catalogues during the dark winter months is an excellent way to plan the coming season's gardening. However, from our own experience, it is easy to get carried away making lists and ordering more seeds than you have time and space to deal with. Do go through your lists a few times, eliminating a few so that you are left with those you really want to raise.

If you are new to growing from seed, start with a selection of varieties that are described as easy, with perhaps just a few more unusual ones. There is nothing like success with your first few packets to give you the confidence to go on and try your skills with more challenging varieties.

INTERNET SITES
In addition to the online shops of the major seed companies, there is a growing number of small websites that specialize in particular types of seed or seed from specific areas. These provide an excellent source of seed not available elsewhere and, provided the appropriate precautions are taken about payment, they are well worth exploring. This is an excellent way of obtaining seeds from other countries, as long as any relevant plant health restrictions are strictly observed. Agricultural and plant health authorities can help you with information on this.

SEED EXCHANGES
Many specialist plant societies, such as the Alpine Garden Society in the UK, and the American Rock Garden Society, run seed exchange schemes for their members. These are

ABOVE **An unknown species of *Oenothera*, raised from wild-collected seed given to us by friends**

usually operated on the basis that members donate seed to the scheme. The seeds are cleaned and packeted by volunteers and a list is then circulated to the membership for them to select the seed they require (this is often restricted to a fixed number of packets). In most schemes the seed is usually free with just a nominal charge to cover postage. These schemes are a good source of seed, often of very rare and unusual varieties, though they are usually on a first-come first-served basis so you are unlikely to receive all your first choices. Substitutes can prove to be just as exciting, as well as unexpected!

However, schemes like this rely on the donors naming the seed accurately. While the vast majority of names will be correct we have had some rather interesting results in which completely different plants were obtained.

SEED COLLECTING EXPEDITIONS

In the past, plants were collected from the wild to be introduced into cultivation, but conservation has quite rightly outlawed this practice, and now introductions are almost exclusively by means of seeds. If you are lucky you may be able to join an expedition run by a specialist society, but for the less adventurous there are several professional seed collectors who sell shares in their expeditions to any interested individuals and organizations. These shares are sold to fund the costs of the expedition and in return the shareholders are sent an allocation of the seeds that are collected. Each expedition is different but most will give an indication of the types of seed they expect to be able to collect given the season and location of the planned seed collecting. So if the plants listed are not of interest you can wait for another trip or try another collector.

ABOVE **Ripened heads of *Fritillaria meleagris*, their seeds ready for collection before they disperse**

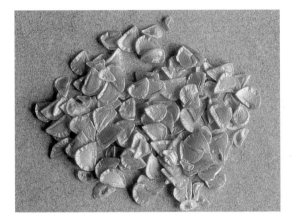

ABOVE **Collected seed of** *Fritillaria meleagris,* **which can just be shaken out of the seed-head**

ABOVE RIGHT **Collecting whole seed-heads into a tray**

RIGHT **Tall stems of seed-heads can be tied in a paper bag to dry**

Growing seed collected in the wild can be very exciting; in some cases, you may be growing plants that are not available in cultivation and in others, you will be growing the original form of a plant which can look completely different to the cultivated forms available from nurseries.

SAVING YOUR OWN SEED

Collecting seed from your own or friends' gardens is a quick way to bulk up many plants. For some more challenging species it can also produce better results as the seed can be sown fresh before any germination inhibitors begin to develop in the seed.

POINTS TO REMEMBER

If you are going to grow plants from your own seed it is important to remember that they will not all come true. In general, a species is much more likely to come true than a hybrid. Most species will come true if they are grown in sufficient isolation from other plants of the same genus.

ABOVE **These seeds can be stripped manually from the seed-heads**

BELOW **A coarse sieve is then used to separate the seed from the chaff**

For instance, to ensure that foxgloves come true it is recommended that they are grown at least 300m (984ft) from another plant of the same genus – difficult to achieve in most gardens!

Sometimes plants with hybrid names will come true from seed, but predictions are very difficult, as every variety is different. The only certainty is that F1 hybrids will not come true from the seed that they produce themselves.

COLLECTING SEEDS

If you are collecting your own seed you need to work with nature and be ready to collect the seed before the plant disperses it itself. Fluffy seed-heads such as *Anemone* or *Pulsatilla* will disappear in the wind as soon as they are ripe, so the plants need to be watched carefully and the seeds collected just before they are ready to disperse. Other plants can be very deceptive and shed their seeds even when the seed-heads still appear to be fresh and green.

Seed needs to be collected from the plant as soon as it is ripe. A good general rule is that if the seed comes away in your hand then it is ready to collect. It may not feel completely dry but, in many cases, if it is left much longer it will disappear, either on the wind or simply fall onto the surrounding soil. If the seed is in a pod or a capsule watch the plant carefully, and as soon as the first pods begin to split start collecting the remaining seeds.

Gather ripened seeds by shaking or cutting off seed-heads into shallow containers or paper bags. With many plants it is often easier to collect the whole seed-head, which can then be placed in a tray until it is dry enough for the seeds to be separated from it. Tall stems can be cut and bundled, the heads placed in a paper bag with the neck tied and then hung upside down by the stems in a cool dry place. As the heads dry, many of the seeds will fall out into the paper bag. Seeds collected this way do not usually need any further cleaning.

Remember to label all seeds as soon as you have collected them.

STORING AND CLEANING SEEDS
STORING SEEDS

When you collect your seeds they will not necessarily be completely dry, particularly if they are collected as complete seed-heads. The surrounding material and the seed-coat need to be dried carefully to ensure rot and fungal diseases do not set in and to help separate out the seed from the surrounding structures, which can be broken up more easily once they are dry. The best way to dry the seeds is to place them in a thin layer in open containers in a dry well-ventilated shed. Some seed-pods and capsules will shoot out their seeds as they dry, so it is best to store these in lidded containers, with the lids propped slightly open, to prevent the seeds escaping. We have found that empty margarine containers are ideal for this and easy to clean out between batches of seed.

The greenhouse is not a good place to dry seeds, as they should not be baked in the sun. High temperatures will dry out the seeds and may damage the embryo, so reducing germination in many species.

Trays of drying seeds are very attractive to mice, so it is a good idea to set some traps around the trays to prevent your seeds being eaten.

Once the seeds are dry then they should be cleaned before being either sown or stored safely for next season.

CLEANING SEEDS

Commercially produced seeds are normally cleaned so that all the surrounding material is removed to leave just the seed itself. This is done for two reasons, one technical and the other commercial! First, the seeds are cleaned to improve germination, as the waste may well rot if left attached to the seed and lead to the seed itself rotting. Second, cleaning improves the presentation of the seed in the packet!

If you are saving your own seed it is important to remove as much waste from around the seed itself, as possible. Fortunately, as you will usually have more than enough seed for sowing, any

ABOVE **A collection of sieves of different mesh sizes**

reduced germination will be more than acceptable compared to the time saved by not producing a pristine seed sample.

Separating and cleaning seeds requires patience, and a variety of methods can be used, depending on the type of seed-head or pod. There are two stages to the cleaning process:

1. Removing the seeds from the seed-head or seed-pod

This is best done as carefully as possible, because the less physical damage to the seed-head, the less chaff will be produced to separate later. Some seeds will simply shake from the seed heads into a tray, while gently rubbing the heads between your fingers will separate all but the most stubborn seeds. Pods of seeds will often split open of their own accord as they dry. Any that have not split can usually be broken open, but if not they may need to be gently crushed until the pod begins to crack.

ABOVE These seeds have fallen easily from the seed-heads

RIGHT Pass seeds through a sieve to separate them from chaff

Some seeds are very firmly held in the pod or capsule and on a small scale the only solution is to separate these individually with tweezers or a blunt needle.

2. Separating the extracted seeds from the chaff

Once the seed-heads have been stripped the resultant seed and debris can often look very similar, so before beginning the separation process it is important to examine everything in detail, making sure you know what is seed and what is chaff before you start. If you are careful you can open a single seed-head before you begin to separate the seed and this will usually allow you to see the colour and shape of the seeds within the structure.

If you cannot do this then look closely at the debris, as this will usually comprise a mixture of uneven shapes, sizes and colours. The seeds will stand out by being an even shape and size – colour is not always a good indicator, as it can vary considerably, even from the same seed-head.

Large seeds such as *Lathyrus* or *Lupinus* can be separated by hand from the chaff. Passing the mix over a series of sieves, each one finer than the previous one, can usually separate the smaller seeds. While it is possible to buy purpose-made seed sieves, these can be

expensive and uneconomic for home-saved seed. We clean our seed using a collection of kitchen sieves, which range in size from large vegetable strainers down to tea strainers and very fine flour sieves. Whatever type of sieve you use it is important to clean it thoroughly between different batches of seed, to ensure no seeds are left in the corners or stuck in the mesh to contaminate future batches.

Begin the sieving process with the largest sieve necessary, working towards the finer mesh, until you reach a size that the seeds will not go through. With very fine seed such as *Campanula* you may find that your sieves are all too coarse and it is not possible to separate the seeds and the fine dust. Unless you are producing a commercial crop it is best to stop at this point or risk losing the fine seeds by attempting further cleaning. We have found most seeds can be cleaned this way, with notable exceptions being very light seeds and long thin ones such as *Tagetes*.

LEFT **The seeds after cleaning**

ABOVE **Store cleaned seeds in waxed envelopes**

Some seeds, such as those of *Anemone,* have very fluffy coats or tails attached – while this can be removed with patience and a delicate touch, on a small scale it is not usually worthwhile, and sowing a little extra seed will make up for any losses caused by rotting.

After sieving, any chaff the same size as the seed can be separated by carefully winnowing the seed. Do this by placing the seed in a shallow tray and carefully blowing over the surface. This will blow away the light chaff leaving the heavier seeds behind. Take care – if you blow too hard the seed will be blown away as well!

SEPARATING SEED FROM FLESHY FRUITS

Seeds with fleshy fruits need to be cleaned carefully and then ideally sown immediately. Cleaning is best done by gently crushing the fruit in a shallow bowl of water. The flesh can then be separated from the fruit mash by careful sieving. Once the seeds have been separated roughly they can be washed again to remove the last remains of the fruit before being sown. If you need to store the seeds they should be dried slowly before placing into waxed bags as with other seeds.

SEED STORAGE

Once the seed has been cleaned it should be placed in a small container that is not completely airtight. We have found that small paper or waxed stamp envelopes are ideal. Care must be taken with paper envelopes as many are not sealed completely at the corners, and you may find that seed can trickle from the gaps. Polythene bags are not a good idea as they can seal in moisture, which will cause the seed to rot in storage. Commercially produced seed is often packed in sealed packets, but this is cleaned and dried in carefully controlled conditions which cannot be reproduced by most gardeners.

The length of time over which seed can be stored varies from species to species but most seeds should last for at least 12 months given good storage conditions. Important exceptions to this are plants (mainly trees) that produce large nut-like seeds, for example *Quercus* and *Aesculus*. These can degenerate very quickly if they dry out and are therefore best sown immediately. Suggested storage times for vegetable seeds are given in chapter 8.

CHAPTER 3

Sowing and germinating seeds

In nature, the odds against a seed being in the right conditions to germinate are very high. Plants have evolved a range of techniques to overcome this and to ensure that at least some seed will germinate to perpetuate the species. Genera such as *Papaver* produce a large number of seeds so that a few will stand a chance of survival, while others produce seeds with hard protective coats to ensure they can survive until the conditions are more favourable for germination. In general, the best way to ensure good germination in the garden is to emulate nature as far as possible, while avoiding adverse conditions at the same time.

CONDITIONS FOR GERMINATION

HYGIENE

If newly sown seed becomes infected with fungal or bacterial disease germination will be reduced, or prevented. Hygiene is crucial, and all containers used for seeds should be new or cleaned and sterilized with a garden disinfectant before use. For almost all seeds, you should also use sterilized compost. If you mix your own compost use new, fresh products and never use material straight from a compost heap.

HEAT, LIGHT AND MOISTURE

Once the seed has been sown, the three most important factors controlling germination are heat,

ABOVE A layer of grit is recommended for covering many seeds, particularly those that are slow to germinate

ABOVE These seedlings have found it difficult to break through the cap, or crust, formed on this compost

ABOVE **Small seedlings easily push their way through this fine grit on the surface**

ABOVE **A selection of pots, seed trays and modular containers used for seed sowing**

ABOVE **Always clean and sterilize old containers before use**

light and moisture. It is generally the case that seeds requiring warmth for germination come from warmer climates; this applies to many of the commonly grown annuals and biennials. These respond to the increasing spring temperatures and germination can be brought forward by exposing them to warmth. Seeds from colder regions, such as many of the alpine plants, need a cold period for germination.

In nature, temperatures fluctuate considerably and this can be a very important factor in aiding germination, except with bedding plants (which have been bred amongst other things to germinate in very controlled conditions). It is therefore important to allow the temperature to fluctuate to simulate natural conditions.

In our experience, the ideal way to germinate seeds of garden plants is to expose them to the natural cycle of the weather in an unheated greenhouse or cold frame.

The amount of light required for germination varies considerably between species. A few species require complete darkness to germinate (*Cyclamen persicum* hybrids being the most common example). Enough light can usually penetrate the surface coverings for most seeds but those that require a greater amount of light, such as celery, are best sown on the surface of

the compost. If you need to cover seeds to retain moisture use a small piece of glass, or a layer of thin polythene. A thin piece of expanded polystyrene will also allow enough light to reach the seeds. Make sure you remove these as soon as germination starts.

SEED COMPOSTS

A good seed compost needs to fulfil the following criteria:

● It must be able to provide you with an even surface, without any lumps and crevices, on which to sow the seed.

● The structure must be open enough to allow the physical movement of water and air but fine enough to allow roots to penetrate freely. Small seeds such as *Campanula* or *Lobelia*, which usually produce very small seedlings, will need much finer compost than larger ones such as *Lathyrus* or *Datura*. An even structure will also make it much easier to separate the seedling roots when it comes to pricking out the seedlings.

● It must be free-draining, yet hold sufficient water for the seed to develop.

● It must have a stable structure that will not break down before the seedlings are pricked out. This is not a problem for seeds that germinate quickly, but can be critical if germination takes a

33

year or more. Cheap peat-based composts are usually the worst and can lose their structure completely within six to nine months.

● It must be easily re-wetted if it dries out; some composts will let water drain through, without any absorption.

● It should be free from diseases and weed seeds. This is best achieved by using fresh compost straight from the bag. Fold over opened

ABOVE **Seeds should be sown thinly and evenly**

ABOVE **This sowing is far too dense and will result in overcrowded seedlings**

ABOVE **These seedlings are evenly spaced and have adequate room to develop**

bags of compost to keep it as sterile as possible. In our experience the best compost is a mix of equal parts of John Innes No.1 and good quality soil-less compost. For slow-to-germinate and moisture-sensitive seeds we usually add an equal amount of fine flint grit. For fast-germinating seeds such as annuals and vegetables the soil-less seed composts available from garden centres are usually very successful although you do need to make sure that they do not dry out in warm weather.

Once the seed has been sown onto the compost surface, we recommend that most seeds are covered with a layer of fine grit or vermiculite rather than compost. This prevents a cap developing, particularly if the seeds take several months to germinate. Using a thin layer of grit or vermiculite will also ensure that some light will be able to penetrate to aid the germination process. Compost can be used on larger seeds such as peas and beans, both of which can easily break through any surface layer. However, always follow specific instructions given on the seed packet, or those for particular plants as discussed in later chapters.

CONTAINERS FOR SOWING SEEDS

Almost any type of container that will hold compost and has drainage holes can be used for seeds. The following are some of the more popular choices.

Seed trays. These are available in several different sizes often helpfully described as full trays at 23x38cm (9x15in), half trays at 18x23cm (7x9in) and quarter trays at 10x18cm (4x7in).

They are also available in a range of different thicknesses. We prefer to use rigid plastic trays as these are easier to move around without disturbing the seeds and, with care, they will last many years. The most useful size for the majority of gardeners is the quarter tray, which is large enough to hold up to about 300 seedlings of most annuals and biennials, more than enough for most gardeners.

We use seed trays for sowing rapidly growing seeds such as annuals and vegetables,

ABOVE **Larger, vigorous seedlings can push their way through a compost layer even if a cap forms**

LEFT **Sowing seed straight from a packet**

RIGHT **Sow large seeds into individual pots, pressing them gently into the compost**

which only spend a short time in the trays. Seeds taking longer to germinate will benefit from deeper containers, which are less likely to dry out during hot spells.

Pots. Pots come in many shapes and sizes, but for seeds small 5–10cm (2–4in) pots are ideal. These are large enough to grow between 20 and 40 seedlings of all but the largest plants. Square pots can be packed together tightly and where space is at a premium are worth the slight extra cost. Terracotta pots are popular with some gardeners, but are best avoided for seeds, as they are difficult to clean and sterilize thoroughly. We use pots for nearly all our seeds, as the extra depth compared to a tray provides a moisture buffer and is also ideal for bulbs and other plants that need to be left to grow in the pot for a season after germination.

For larger quantities of seed we have found that dwarf pots, sometimes sold as half pots, are very useful. These are 14cm (5.5in) diameter with a depth of 9cm (3.5in).

Modular containers. There are many different types of modular container or cell trays available, normally made from various types of plastic and sometimes from expanded polystyrene. As with seed trays we prefer the more rigid types, as these are easier to handle and last much longer. Expanded polystyrene is not ideal, as many more vigorous seedlings will root into the material itself resulting in considerable root damage when the plants

are removed. The big advantage of modular containers is that they remove the need to prick out the seedlings. By sowing one large seed or a pinch of small seeds per cell, the seedlings can be left to develop until they are at the planting-out stage.

Peat containers. These are pots made of compressed peat, which becomes porous once wet and filled with compost, allowing the seedlings to root into the pot itself. This is then planted straight into the ground or into a larger pot when the seedling is ready. These pots do, however, require very careful management as the pot itself must always be kept wet. As soon as the peat dries out any roots growing into it will die, resulting in a check to the growth of the plant. Keep them packed together closely in a tray if possible.

Recycled containers. Provided these have drainage holes cut in them all sorts of containers can work very well. Care is required with transparent containers as these will allow light to reach the compost around the edges and this can check the growth of any roots near the edge of the container.

STERILIZING CONTAINERS

Whatever type of container you choose it must be clean and preferably sterilized. Wherever possible we use new pots, which are then used again for potting on. It is important to sterilize old containers with garden disinfectant or the disinfectant solutions sold for babies' bottles etc. Whichever type you use, follow the instructions and make sure the containers are dry before you sow the seeds.

FILLING THE CONTAINERS

Fill pots with compost to within 1cm (½in), and seed trays to within 6mm (¼in), of the tops. Lightly firm the compost, using either a piece of wood cut to fit the container, or the base of a similar clean container. Press just sufficiently to level the surface of the compost without compressing it. Place in a tray of water and allow the water to soak up through the compost until the surface appears just moist.

SOWING IN CONTAINERS

Achieving an even spread of seeds is one of the keys to successful seed growing especially with large numbers of seeds. Seedlings need to emerge evenly with adequate space to grow and develop before pricking on. Too dense a sowing will result in drawn, weak seedlings, which are difficult to separate at pricking out time, and are very prone to diseases such as damping off and greymould (botrytis).

To sow small quantities of seed in pots, place the seeds in the hand and gently tap from a slightly bent palm over the compost. Larger quantities can be readily sown straight from the packets provided the corner is cut off to form a spout. You can then gently shake the seed over the container while moving steadily from side to side across it. The most even results are obtained by sowing the seed in both directions across the container (half the quantity in each direction).

Sow larger seeds individually by spacing them evenly over the surface of the container and pressing gently into the compost so they are level with the surface.

Very large seeds such as beans or many of the squashes are ideally sown individually into 7cm (3in) pots. Do this by gently pressing the seed into the compost to a depth equal to the size of the seed, then level off the compost to cover the seed.

Modular trays have a small surface area and it is a good idea to make a shallow impression in the centre of each cell so that the seeds fall to the centre rather than around the edges. If they are large enough to handle, seeds can be sown individually into the cells, but sow smaller seeds such as lettuce or cabbage from the palm, as described above, tapping just a few into each cell. The resultant clump of seedlings can either be left to develop or thinned out early on to leave just one strong one to grow on.

Once your seed has been sown, cover with either vermiculite or fine grit. Both are easier to apply if they are dry, and for most seeds a covering of about 6mm (¼in) should be ideal. Seeds that need light to germinate, such as celery and many of the primulas, can be covered with a very thin layer just to anchor them.

ABOVE **A wooden cold frame with lift-up lids**

ABOVE **This greenhouse bench can hold plenty of pots of seeds**

ABOVE **For sowing outside, first rake the soil level**

ABOVE **Use a blunt cane to make a shallow furrow**

ABOVE **Water the furrow before sowing the seeds**

ABOVE **Sow seeds fairly thinly and evenly**

ABOVE **Gently push the soil over the seeds using the back of the rake**

ABOVE **Label the rows and water using a fine rose on a watering can**

Alternatively, just lightly press the seeds into the surface of the compost. As mentioned earlier, you can cover larger, more vigorous seeds with compost, as these will readily force their way through any cap that forms.

There are several different types of seed-sowing aid available from garden centres and shops, but we have yet to find one that is more reliable than the methods described above. The simpler devices consist of a plastic container with a spout and a range of holes to control the flow of seed, so if you have unsteady hands these are worth a try.

STRUCTURES FOR GERMINATION

To germinate seeds successfully it is not necessary to have expensive or complicated facilities. Many seeds will germinate freely if left in a sheltered place in the garden, but results can be improved by providing even the simplest additional protection. The most important thing is to prevent the seed containers becoming waterlogged during prolonged wet weather. Do this by supporting a rigid cover several inches above the containers. Beyond this a range of structures can be used, depending on the space available and the type of seeds you wish to grow.

Cold frames. These are available from garden centres in many different shapes and sizes or, if you are handy with a screwdriver and saw, you can easily build one yourself. It must be possible to ventilate the frame in hot weather. In our experience, the best have lids that lift from the front and slope backwards. Designs where the lid slides up or down can be a problem if there is a sudden unexpected shower as even moderate rain can generate a big enough flow of water to wash compost and seeds from any containers beneath the edge. Frames with solid sides are ideal for germinating seeds but to prevent the seedlings becoming drawn towards the light the containers will need to be moved once the seedlings appear. This problem does not occur with glass-sided frames. Whatever

type of frame you use it should be situated in a light position, but preferably shaded from the heat of the midday sun.

Greenhouses. An unheated greenhouse bench would be our first choice for germinating seeds, as it will provide the same protection from wet weather as a cold frame, with the added advantage of allowing you to easily monitor the progress of the seeds. The greenhouse should have plenty of ventilation, and windows should be kept partially open in all but the most extreme weather. In summer, shading the outside of the greenhouse will help to keep the temperature down, particularly important for young seedlings, which can scorch quickly.

Propagators. In their simplest form these are no more than a clear plastic lid designed to fit over a seed tray, usually with a simple vent in the lid. If space is limited these simple propagators can be used instead of a cold frame and placed in a sheltered spot in the garden. Ideally, however, they are best used in a cold greenhouse.

Another type of propagator consists of a base (a tray) containing a heating element. A clear cover retains the warmth generated. This is ideal for seeds that need a higher temperature to germinate, such as annual bedding plants and many houseplants. It can either be purchased ready-made from garden centres or as a kit to make your own. If you do not have electricity connected to your greenhouse, small models are available, designed to fit on a house windowsill. These work well provided the seedlings are potted on quickly, to prevent them becoming drawn by the one-sided light.

Heated propagators are useful when a constant temperature is needed. However, some seeds, particularly perennials, trees and shrubs, benefit from fluctuations in temperature. We have found that placing the containers of seeds in a heated propagator without the cover is ideal, as the heated base provides warmth but fluctuations occur due to the temperature changes in the surrounding greenhouse.

ABOVE **On coarse lumpy soil, rake down as much as possible**

ABOVE **Using a trowel, make a shallow trench**

SOWING IN THE OPEN GROUND

Sowing seeds directly into the garden soil can be a very successful way to establish certain plants, particularly annuals and many vegetables. Root vegetables such as carrots and parsnips will produce forked and therefore useless roots if they are damaged during transplanting.

PREPARING THE SOIL

To ensure good germination it is important to prepare the soil well before sowing. If you have a heavy clay soil, it is a good idea to dig in plenty of compost, preferably in the autumn, leaving the soil untouched over the winter, when alternate freezing and thawing will help to break down the lumps. Provided the soil is moist but not wet it can then be gently raked over in the spring to produce a fine seedbed. The finer the seed you intend to sow the finer the seedbed should be.

SOWING OUTDOORS

Hardy annuals, such as *Calendula* and *Papaver*, are best sown in blocks or drifts, broadcasting the seeds evenly over the surface. Sow the seeds more thickly than in a seed tray as germination will usually be lower due to effects of the weather and soil pests and diseases. Once broadcast, cover the seed by lightly raking the surface or sprinkling a fine covering of sand over the seeds – this has the additional advantage of clearly marking the area that has been sown. Seeds of vegetables are usually best sown in rows. Make a shallow furrow in the soil surface. There are many ways to do this but we prefer to use a blunt cane, which makes a neat, uncompacted furrow with a fine tilth in the base.

If the seedbed is very coarse and lumpy it is a good idea to make a shallow trench with a hoe and then fill this with John Innes compost in which you can make your seed furrow. (Avoid using soil-less composts as these can dry out very quickly and prevent germination.)

If the soil is very dry at sowing time it is also a good idea to carefully water the base of the furrow before you sow your seeds so they have moist soil all around them.

Seeds sown directly into the soil are vulnerable to many different problems. Cover the seedbed with cloches to control the effects of the weather; traditional glass barn cloches are very effective, but modern plastic structures are easier and safer to handle. Many different cloches are available and the choice is more down to appearance and the depth of your pocket! Home-made structures can also be very effective.

Birds can be major pests in some areas – they either search for the newly sown seeds or graze the newly germinated seedlings. We have found that horticultural fleece laid over the seedbed is very effective in preventing this while allowing the seedlings to develop unrestricted.

ABOVE **Fill the trench with John Innes compost**

ABOVE **Make a furrow in the compost to sow the seeds into**

TIMING OF SOWING

Seeds that germinate freely will do so at most times of the year, but timing becomes important when subsequent growth is considered. For example, annuals normally flower from late spring through to early autumn, so there is little point sowing seeds in the summer to get flowering-size plants by the autumn when the weather conditions will not allow them to flower!

The same is true of many vegetables, which need a period of time to develop before cropping. If they are sown too late they may well grow but you will not get a crop.

Early sowing can also cause problems, as seedlings developing early in the season may well need additional protection or extra heat to keep them growing. In our experience it is usually better to sow at the recommended time so the plants can be kept growing steadily. These can often outperform the earlier-grown, forced plants.

If you buy commercially produced seed, suggested sowing times are usually marked on the packet. If you are collecting your own seed, then follow the guidelines in chapters 5 to 9.

GERMINATION TREATMENTS

In order to germinate successfully, some seeds need to be subjected to a range of physical and environmental conditions before the process begins. Wherever possible, as discussed earlier, we prefer to do this by sowing the seeds in pans and exposing them to the natural weather cycle. For some seeds, such as *Alstroemeria*, artificial treatment produces better results.

Cold treatment. Seeds such as alpines, which originate from cold climates, will often benefit from a period at a low temperature of about 1–3°C (34–38°F). This can be achieved by using a normal domestic refrigerator.

For the treatment to be effective the seeds must be moist – simply storing the dry seed packets in the fridge will not be sufficient. The best way of achieving success is by mixing the seed with a small quantity of moist vermiculite, in a polythene bag, then sealing it and placing it in the refrigerator. Temperatures below freezing should be avoided as they can have the reverse effect and slow the germination process.

Stratification. This process is effective with many tree and shrub seeds, as it closely resembles their natural germination cycle. Collect the seeds and fruits as soon as they are ripe and place them in polythene bags with moist vermiculite. Then place these in a sealed container on the shelf of an unheated shed, and examine the bags regularly.

As soon as you see the first signs of germination, remove the seeds and sow them carefully in containers. To be successful the process needs to be started as soon as possible to ensure the seeds receive the same cycle of conditions they would do naturally.

CHAPTER 4

Care of seeds after sowing

By taking care of your newly sown seeds you are much more likely to achieve success. This applies to seeds that need long germination periods as much as to those that germinate almost immediately.

WATERING SEEDS

Once the seeds have been sown in the ground or in containers they should be watered thoroughly to settle the soil or compost around them. Watering should be done very carefully. The traditional technique of using an upturned fine rose on a watering can is very effective, as the resultant gentle spray of water ensures that the topping is not disturbed and the seeds are not washed away. Alternatively, stand the pots or trays in a container of water so that they take up moisture gradually, and from the base. Remove them once the surface becomes moist.

After their initial watering, seeds sown in containers should be watered sparingly so the compost is kept just moist and never becomes waterlogged. The best way to judge when to water containers topped with grit is to lift the containers, and it becomes easy to judge from the weight when they need more water. Seed containers placed outside are best under some form of overhead cover to protect them from heavy rainfall. They can always be watered if they become dry but it is very difficult to quickly dry out waterlogged compost.

Once seeds begin to germinate it is essential that they are not allowed to dry out. Whenever possible, watering should be done either in the early morning, which gives the seedling leaves a chance

ABOVE Avoid drips when watering by tipping the can up away from the seed tray

RIGHT Then move the water spray over the seed tray

ABOVE Success with germinating seeds is more achievable if they are given care and attention

to dry before the heat of the sun can scorch them, or early evening, which prevents them remaining moist overnight. We have found that with very small seedlings, such as those of many alpine plants, it is best to use a fine spray from a small hand sprayer to prevent damage to the delicate seedlings.

IMPORTANCE OF CLEAN WATER

Seeds and seedlings must always be watered from a tap or a clean storage tank. Rainwater stored in water-butts is not clean, as in running off a roof or other surface it will pick up bacteria, spores of various fungi, and particularly mosses and algae. These are then spread over the compost by watering and can result in the death of the seeds or at best the development of a green layer on the surface of the container. We find that the cleanliness of tap water far outweighs any slight problems that might be caused by any additives in it. We have always had very hard water and have found that this does not cause a problem, even with seeds of ericaceous plants.

SIGNS OF GERMINATION

The first signs of germination vary considerably. With large seeds, such as beans, the surface of the compost becomes disturbed and raised

ABOVE **Use clean water from a tap to water seeds**

ABOVE **The first signs of germination are always exciting!**

RIGHT **Tomato seedlings raised in a pot**

before the seedling appears, whereas with small seeds tiny green specks may appear among the grit. These enlarge slowly as the seedling leaves become visible. You need to inspect seed sowings regularly for signs of germination – as well as the anticipation of seeing new seedlings emerging, you can monitor their progress and apply any appropriate treatment needed.

Many seeds will germinate slowly over several weeks or even months. Others, particularly varieties that have been developed commercially such as many bedding plants and vegetables, will germinate in a very short time, often no longer than two to three days.

This is an exciting time as some of your seeds start to develop into new plants, so give them the care and attention they need to thrive.

SEEDLING PROBLEMS

The following are the main things to watch out for as your seedlings start to grow. With regular inspections and attention to detail, you should avoid many of them.

Damping off. This is one of the most common problems. The symptoms usually begin with the seedlings flopping or collapsing, often with some discolouration to the stem. In some cases, a fluffy growth can be seen on the seedlings or the

ABOVE **Newly germinating *Arum* seedlings**

compost. The symptoms can progress very rapidly with a whole pot of seedlings being destroyed in a couple of days. Damping off is caused by a variety of soil- and water-borne fungi. These can also infect seeds before they germinate causing patchy emergence or no emergence at all.

The problem normally develops when seedlings are over-wet and are being kept in temperatures

ABOVE Seedlings of *Ipomoea* (morning glory) are relatively large — these are the seedling leaves

that are too warm. Sowing seeds too densely can also be a contributing factor. Closely spaced, weak seedlings do not allow free air circulation and the air around them remains very moist.

Poor hygiene invites infection, so containers used for seeds should either be new or sterilized, and new, sterile compost should always be used. As mentioned earlier, watering should only be done with clean tap water and not from rainwater-butts.

Damping off can be difficult to control once it appears. Moving the seeds to drier, less humid conditions sometimes helps, as does drenching the compost with a copper-based fungicide. If healthy seedlings are large enough to handle they should be pricked out as soon as possible into clean compost and containers, and kept in a well-ventilated position until they become established.

ABOVE **These seedlings have become tall and spindly due to the seeds being sown too densely**

Dense sowing. As well as increasing the risk of damping off, sowing seeds too densely causes them to become thin and spindly, as they fight for limited light and space, and they also end up with very tangled root systems. These weak seedlings are easily damaged during pricking out and they seldom establish well.

Space large seeds out well and sow smaller seeds thinly. Use more containers rather than sowing too thickly, as the results will always be better than trying to pack too many seeds into small containers.

Mice. In the greenhouse, mice are usually more of a problem in the winter months when they come inside looking for easy food. In our experience they will dig out and eat almost any seeds, even those as small as brassica seeds. There are many different types of mousetraps on the market, and whichever you choose it should be small enough to place across the top edges of containers as traps placed on the surrounding bench are never as effective. An alternative is to cover the seeds with a fine metal mesh about 1cm (½in) square which will prevent all but the smallest mice digging in your containers.

In the open ground mice tend to be attracted to larger seeds such as peas and beans. Trapping can be effective but is much more difficult because of the larger areas involved. Covering sown areas with mesh or netting may help to deter them.

ABOVE **Damping off causes seedlings to collapse, destroying many in this tray**

ABOVE Mousetraps are useful on pots of seeds to prevent rodents digging into them

RIGHT A cloche covered in horticultural fleece can deter flea beetles

Flea beetles. These are small beetles about 2mm (1/12in) long, which eat small holes in the surface of the leaves, particularly in seedlings, though older plants can also be attacked. A bad attack can kill young seedlings, and even a mild problem makes the leaves unsightly, especially in leaf crops such as Pak Choi. Plants of the brassica family can be particularly badly hit. The beetles are active in mid-spring to late summer.

A good way to avoid bad attacks is to sow susceptible seeds only when conditions allow the seedlings to grow away rapidly. Keep the seedlings well watered in dry weather to allow them to grow away from any attack.

We have found that covering seeds with horticultural fleece is also very effective, creating a physical barrier to prevent damage.

Chemical treatments can be used if necessary, following the manufacturers' instructions carefully. Those containing derris or pirimiphos-methyl are usually very effective.

Slugs and snails. These have voracious appetites for young seedlings. The damage they cause can range from holes in the edges and centre of leaves of large seedlings such as beans to the complete consumption of smaller seedlings.

Both of these molluscs can be readily controlled with the various brands of slug pellets available, but non-chemical methods can be just as effective.

47

ABOVE **Slug damage on a coleus seedling – slugs and snails can devour whole seedlings in no time**

Outdoors, the use of sharp grit as a top dressing is unpleasant to the soft bodies of slugs, making a good deterrent. The grit should be placed around the seedlings or along each side of the row to discourage slugs. In greenhouses and cold frames slug traps baited with liquid such as beer can be very effective.

In the garden, treating the seedbed with nematodes – a biological control that infects and kills the slugs – is another effective method. The nematodes can be applied in the spring once the soil temperature rises above 5°C (41°F). They will remain active for up to six weeks if the compost is kept moist.

Rabbits and birds. These are usually only a problem with outdoor sowings in beds. Birds are known to eat some seeds; they also love pecking around in freshly dug soil and in so doing can throw newly sown seeds around. The best protection is normally to place netting over and around the seedbed. To keep out rabbits the netting should be fixed firmly to the ground.

Moss and liverworts. These can develop on containers of seeds, particularly those that take several months to germinate. If left uncontrolled they will form an impenetrable mat preventing the seeds from germinating. Using a topping of grit on the containers will help to prevent the growth of moss and liverwort as it keeps the surface of the pot dry (both need moisture to develop). Using water collected from a roof will cause mosses to develop very quickly and

ABOVE **Wire netting can keep birds and rabbits away from outdoor seedbeds**

ABOVE Mosses develop by using unclean water and will inhibit germination or limit seedling growth

RIGHT Leave seedlings of bulbous plants, such as this *Fritillaria*, to develop for a season before potting on

should always be avoided. If growth does begin it should be carefully removed as soon as possible to prevent it spreading.

Sun scorch. During spells of hot weather young seedlings are very prone to scorching from the bright sun, particularly if they are growing in greenhouses and cold frames. The seedlings should be lightly shaded, by covering the glass with a layer of shade netting. This is preferable to using paint-on treatments, as it can be removed easily during spells of dull weather.

Weeds. Weeds occur in the best kept gardens and weed seeds can creep into seed pans from a variety of sources. If you are new to growing it can be difficult to distinguish weed seeds from your precious seedlings, particularly in the early

stages. One good clue is to look and see if the same seedlings are appearing in pots of several different seeds! If you are unsure wait a few days and often the intended seedlings will emerge, making the rogues obvious. Weed seedlings should be removed as soon as possible. Dig them out carefully with a dibber or small fork, taking care to disturb as little of the surrounding compost as possible.

49

ABOVE **The correct way to handle a seedling is to hold it by a leaf**

ABOVE **Never hold a seedling by its stem**

PRICKING OUT SEEDLINGS

Almost all seedlings should be pricked out as soon as possible, ideally when they have just begun to develop their first true leaves. The main exceptions to this are seedlings of most bulbous plants, which should really be left to develop for a season. By this time they will have grown tiny bulbs which will grow away rapidly in the second season.

The pricking out, or transplanting stage, is one of the most critical in the life of young seedlings. They have very soft tissues, which are easily damaged, so seedlings should always be handled by their leaves, and NEVER by the stem. They will develop more leaves if these are damaged, but they will not produce another stem and damage to this will cause rapid death.

CONTAINERS TO USE

Each time a seedling is transplanted, its growth receives a check while the roots re-establish themselves in the new compost. Traditionally, many seedlings were pricked out into trays before being transplanted after a few weeks into pots, then later being planted into the soil or a larger container. In our experience it is better, wherever possible, to miss out at least one stage and prick out larger seedlings directly into pots in which they develop until they are large enough to plant out or pot into their final containers.

Many annuals and vegetables can be pricked out into cell trays. Trays with cells of 3cm (1¼in) or more in diameter will allow the seedlings to develop compact root systems which will be strong enough for planting directly into their final growing positions.

Seed trays can also be used for pricking out. Seedlings need to be given plenty of space to develop in the tray and should be spaced at least 2.5cm (1in) apart in each direction.

COMPOST TO USE

Seedlings should ideally be pricked out into compost containing slightly higher levels of nutrient than that used for sowing seeds. It is

ABOVE **These lettuces have been transplanted from modules into the open ground and are growing strongly**

better, particularly for small seedlings, to use a seed compost and to feed the seedlings with dilute liquid feed once they begin to grow away rapidly. Fill the container with compost, level it off with the top edge, and tap gently on the potting bench to settle it.

HANDLING SEEDLINGS

Loosen the compost around the seedlings prior to pricking out, in order to minimize damage to the roots. Tip pots of seedlings carefully out onto the bench, or loosen the compost in seed trays by gently tapping the tray on the bench. The seed compost should be moist when you prick out, but the seedling leaves are easier to handle if they are dry – so water the pots or trays a few hours before you start, to allow the foliage time to dry.

Ease the delicate seedlings from the compost using a small fork or a dibber, taking care to damage the roots as little as possible. Any compost on the roots should be left attached to minimize damage to the fine root hairs. For the best results choose short stocky seedlings, avoiding any that have become tall and spindly.

Even though the former may appear small initially, they will establish more rapidly and produce a stronger, more vigorous plant.

Using a dibber, make a hole in the compost and, holding the seedling by the leaves, gently lower the roots in. Use the dibber to guide the roots into the hole but not to push them into the compost. Plant the seedling so the compost level on the stem is the same as it was in the seed container. Gently firm the compost around the roots sufficiently to support the seedling. Finally, water the compost well and place the plants in a lightly shaded position until they have settled down and begun to develop.

Seedlings of some plants, such as *Lobelia* and *Exacum*, are very small and difficult to handle individually. Good results can be achieved with these by transplanting them in small clumps, which results not only in a robust 'plant' but also means that if one has been damaged the others can grow away and its loss will not be noticed. This works well with seedlings of the same flower colour but can produce some interesting results if you are using a packet of mixed colours!

Large seedlings, such as those of some trees and shrubs, are likely to have well-developed root systems. These are usually best transplanted by half-filling the pot with compost, and then, holding the seedling in place by its leaves, filling the pot carefully with compost around the roots. This method spreads the root system out and allows it to develop with only a minimum check.

Water the seedlings thoroughly and place in a cool, shaded place. Some seedlings will wilt once they have been transplanted, but will usually be standing up again within 24 hours. Any that have not recovered within 48 hours have been damaged in pricking out and should be discarded. If they are in seed or cell trays the dead seedlings should be carefully removed to prevent them attracting disease which could then spread to the healthy seedlings.

SEEDLINGS IN OPEN GROUND

Seeds that have been sown into the garden soil, if they need transplanting, are normally moved straight into their growing positions in the garden. Prepare the area in which they are going to be planted by digging it over well, breaking down the soil to a medium tilth. Lift the seedlings using a trowel and carefully separate if necessary. In our experience the best way to plant them is to dig a hole with a trowel deep enough to accommodate the roots, then hold the seedling in place by its leaves and carefully fill the hole, firming the soil lightly to support the seedling. Water the seedlings thoroughly – this will also help to settle the soil around the roots. The seedlings may wilt very quickly but, as mentioned earlier, they will usually show signs of recovery within 24 hours.

With larger seedlings, such as brassicas, the growing tip will usually recover while the older seedling leaves will eventually wither and die. On exposed sites or in windy weather, a covering of horticultural fleece will help the seedlings to recover and establish more rapidly.

FAR LEFT **A pot of seedlings ready to prick out into a modular tray**

ABOVE LEFT **Tip the pot out and separate the seedlings gently with a dibber**

BELOW LEFT **Make a hole in the compost using the dibber and lower the seedling in**

RIGHT **The finished, labelled tray – the seedlings will soon straighten up**

AFTERCARE OF SEEDLINGS AND HARDENING OFF

If the seedlings are well watered when they are pricked out, it may be several days before they need more water. The compost should be kept moist but not too wet. As the seedlings begin to develop the amount of shading can be gradually reduced although care will still be required on hot days.

If the seedlings have been pricked out into a seed compost, begin feeding after about 10 to 14 days. Use a dilute solution of liquid feed, following the manufacturers' instructions carefully. Liquid feed should be applied either on dull days or in the evening to prevent the leaves being scorched. Do not overfeed young seedlings or they will grow too soft, encouraging fungal diseases.

Seedlings that have been grown in a greenhouse or cold frame need to be gradually acclimatized or 'hardened off' from the protected environment in which they have developed. The easiest way to do this is to gradually increase the ventilation in the cold frame, leaving the lid further and further open each day, but closing it down at night. After about a week the plants should by hardened enough to be moved outside to a sheltered area.

Plants being grown in a greenhouse can initially be moved nearer to the ventilator, and then to a sheltered spot outside for a period each day until after about a week they are left outside all day and night. Early in the season, seedlings of many annuals and tender plants are still susceptible to frost and they should be protected with a layer of horticultural fleece if light frosts – down to -2°C (29°F) – are forecast, or moved back inside if severe frost is forecast.

Your seedlings are ready for planting out or potting on as soon as they have developed a good root system. The first sign of this is usually the appearance of roots coming out of the holes at the base of the container. Plants in pots can be carefully tipped out, and if they are ready to plant they should show an even spread of roots around the compost. The rootball should feel firm, due to the development of roots inside the compost. Plants in cells can usually be examined in a similar way, by carefully pushing a single plant out of its cell.

CHAPTER 5

Annuals and biennials from seed

WHAT ARE ANNUALS AND BIENNIALS?

An annual is a plant that completes its entire life cycle during one year. Germination, growth, flowering and seed production all take place within one year and the plant then dies. Annuals are classed as 'hardy' if they can withstand a certain amount of frost, and 'half-hardy' if they are intolerant of frost.

A biennial, on the other hand, is a plant requiring two seasons to complete its life cycle. In the first year, germination takes place and leaves grow. The plant overwinters and then flowers and produces seeds in the second year, before it dies. Biennials are usually sown in early summer so that the plants can become well established enough to survive the winter outside.

Some perennial plants – which survive from year to year – are best treated as annuals, either because they are tender, or they are naturally short-lived. When grown as if they were annuals, by being raised from seed and then discarded at the end of the season, they are vigorous and free-flowering, capable of producing blooms quickly from seed sown in spring. They give a much poorer performance, however, if left to continue for further seasons. Geraniums, gazanias and busy lizzies are all perennials that are treated as annuals.

USES IN THE GARDEN

Annuals are traditionally used in gardens to achieve colour quickly, fairly cheaply and in abundance. Many produce a profusion of flowers over several weeks, sometimes months, creating lots of colour either in borders or containers. Although short-lived, some can put on an incredible amount of growth, even in one season, so they can be very effective at filling in gaps in borders. Alternatively, you can create a whole bed of annuals and biennials, particularly those with varying growth habits and a range of foliage and flowers.

Annuals are useful for trying out new colour schemes, experimenting to see if a particular colour is pleasing in a specific spot or suitable for the effect you want to achieve. If the experiment is successful you could then substitute the annuals later, perhaps the following year, with permanent plants, such as shrubs or herbaceous perennials, in the same colour.

Because they provide an instant effect, annuals are ideal for new gardens. You can also change them during the season for a different display – some annuals flower later than others, so you can discard the earlier ones and substitute fresh ones.

Many annuals, such as pansies and petunias, are available in a wide range of colours, both bright and muted. They blend, therefore, with all sorts of colour schemes. Because they can be raised or bought inexpensively, you can use them in larger numbers to give blocks or drifts of colour.

ABOVE *Antirrhinum* 'Night & Day'

GROWING REQUIREMENTS

Many annuals can be sown directly outside in the place where they are to flower. Sowing usually takes place in spring. These annuals are mostly easy to grow from seed, growing relatively quickly, although it is important to get them off to a good start by preparing the ground thoroughly. Once sown, the area needs to be kept watered so that the seedlings are not checked in their growth. Remove weed seedlings as soon as they appear, to reduce competition for water, nutrients and light.

Groups of annuals can be grown successfully among other plants, or in small beds on their own. Alternatively, they can be sown in drills or patches in the potager or kitchen garden, where suitable forms can be grown to provide flowers for cutting.

Annuals do not generally require any special seed treatments, so sowing directly outside is a simple and effective way of raising the majority of them. Most have rapid germination rates, and many annuals available today have been bred for uniformity and commercial production, so they germinate both rapidly and evenly. Most annual seeds are, however, best sown outside only when the weather, and therefore the soil, begins to warm up.

There are some annuals that need rather more care during germination and early seedling growth. The seeds of petunias and impatiens, for example, need moist, humid conditions in which to germinate, and this is far more easily achieved and maintained in a greenhouse or propagator than outdoors in the soil. Annuals such as antirrhinums and petunias are slow growing when at the seedling stage, so these can be monitored more closely when grown under cover.

Sowing under cover also means the seeds can be sown much earlier, with some heat, so that the young plants are advanced enough and ready to put out when all danger of frost is over. Annuals can also be sown inside to give them a

ABOVE **Seeds of *Aster* 'Matsumoto'**

head start in spring and a longer flowering season. Care must be taken not to sow fast-germinating and fast-growing annuals too early, as they will grow too tall and leggy before conditions are suitable for planting out, and they will transplant less well in this state.

Sowing inside is also recommended for cold areas, or the growing season may be too short.

POPULAR ANNUALS AND BIENNIALS

These are some of the popular types grown in gardens, with details of sowing and any specific requirements. For each type, we have suggested two or three named hybrids or seed mixtures available from commercial seed suppliers. These can be purchased directly from seed firms by mail order, or can be found in many garden centres or shops. It is worth obtaining seed catalogues to see the range offered, as many are pictured and you can make your own selection. Those sown directly outside will germinate best when the soil warms up to 8–12°C (46–54°F).

NAME: *ANTIRRHINUM* (SNAPDRAGON)
TYPE: **HALF-HARDY ANNUAL**

Sowing time: Mid-winter to early spring inside
Temperature: 15–21°C (59–70°F)
Germination time: 7–21 days
Specific notes: Seedlings are slow growing, so start early by sowing seed under protected conditions. Many antirrhinums are hybrids so if you collect your own seed, plants will vary in colour and quality
Examples: 'Night & Day' 45cm (18in); 'Black Prince' 45cm (18in); 'Magic Carpet Mixed' 15cm (6in). Flowering early summer to autumn

NAME: *ASTER*
TYPE: **HALF-HARDY ANNUAL**

Sowing time: Early to mid-spring inside or mid to late spring direct outside
Optimum temperature: 18–20°C (66–68°F) under glass
Germination time: 7–21 days
Specific notes: Annual asters can be prone to a wilt disease, causing the sudden collapse of seedlings or young plants. Some varieties have improved resistance to this
Examples: *Aster chinensis* 'Milady Mixed' 25cm (10in); 'Matsumoto' series (cut flower Japanese asters) 75cm (30in). Flowering early summer to mid-autumn

NAME: *CALENDULA* (POT MARIGOLD)
TYPE: **HARDY ANNUAL**

Sowing time: Late winter inside or spring outside. Can also be sown outside early autumn to overwinter for earlier flowering
Optimum temperature: 18–20°C (66–68°F) under glass
Germination time: 4–21 days
Specific notes: Very quick and easy to grow
Examples: 'Greenheart Orange' 45–60cm (18–24in); 'Indian Prince' 75cm (30in); 'Pink Surprise' 60cm (24in). Flowering early summer to mid-autumn

NAME: *CENTAUREA* (CORNFLOWER)
TYPE: **HARDY ANNUAL**

Sowing time: Spring outside, or early autumn outside for flowering the following year
Optimum temperature: 10–12°C (50–54°F)
Germination time: 10–14 days
Specific notes: Easy to grow, with rapid germination outside. Will also self-seed
Examples: *C. cyanus* 'Tall Mixed' 90cm (36in); *C. cyanus* 'Black Ball' 75cm (30in); *C. moschata* 'The Bride' 40–60cm (16–24in). Flowering mid-summer to early autumn

ABOVE **Seeds of** *Cosmos* **'Polidor Mixed'**

NAME: *COSMOS*
TYPE: **HALF-HARDY ANNUAL**

Sowing time: Late winter to mid-spring inside, or mid to late spring outside
Optimum temperature: 18–21°C (66–70°F) inside, 15–18°C (59–66°F) outside
Germination time: 3–10 days
Specific notes: Exposure to light is beneficial for germination, so leave seed uncovered
Examples: *C. bipinnatus* 'Daydream' 90cm (36in); *C. bipinnatus* 'Seashells' 90cm (36in); 'Sonata Mixed' 60cm (24in). Flowering mid-summer to mid-autumn

NAME: *DAHLIA*
TYPE: **HALF-HARDY ANNUAL**
(HHP TREATED AS HHA)

Sowing time: Mid-winter to mid-spring inside
Optimum temperature: 15–20°C (59–68°F)
Germination time: 7–14 days
Specific notes: Seed germinates quickly and seedlings grow quite rapidly so don't sow too early. Wide colour range; dwarf bedding types to taller ones for cutting
Examples: 'Figaro Mixed' 30cm (12in); 'Diablo Mixed' 38cm (15in); 'Collarette Dandy' 50–60cm (20–24in). Flowering mid-summer to mid-autumn

NAME: *DIANTHUS* (PINKS)
TYPE: **HARDY ANNUAL**

Sowing time: Late winter to early spring inside
Optimum temperature: 18–21°C (66–70°F)
Germination time: 7–10 days
Specific notes: Cover seed with a thin layer of vermiculite. Once germinated place in cooler conditions, say 10°C (50°F), and keep seedlings in good light for early flowering
Examples: Annual pinks are mostly *D. chinensis* or hybrids of *D. heddewigii*. 'Black & White Minstrels' 30–38cm (12–15in); 'Baby Doll Mixed' 15cm (6in); 'Strawberry Parfait' 15cm (6in). Flowering mid-summer to mid-autumn

LEFT *Dianthus barbatus* (Sweet William)

NAME: *DIANTHUS BARBATUS* (SWEET WILLIAM)
TYPE: HARDY BIENNIAL

Sowing time: Sowing should take place from late spring to early summer outside
Optimum temperature: 12–15°C (54–59°F)
Germination time: 14–21 days
Specific notes: Thin out where sown, or transplant in late summer if sown in rows elsewhere. Can also sow into large modules in cold frame, then plant out when established
Examples: 'Monarch Mixed' 45cm (18in); 'Duplex Mixture' 55cm (22in); 'Auricula Eyed' 45cm (18in). Flowering late spring to mid-summer the year after sowing

NAME: *DIGITALIS* (FOXGLOVE)
TYPE: HARDY BIENNIAL

Sowing time: Mid-spring to early summer direct outside, or late winter to late spring in pots or modules in cold frame
Optimum temperature: 10–15°C (50–59°F)
Germination time: 14–30 days
Specific notes: Cover the very fine seed only lightly. Take care with seeds – toxic if eaten

Examples: *D. purpurea* 'Alba', 'Apricot' or 'Excelsior Hybrid Mixed' 1.2–1.5m (4–5ft), all forms bred from the common foxglove; *D. x mertonensis* 75cm (30in); *D. grandiflora* 90cm (36in). Flowering late spring to mid-summer

NAME: *GERANIUM (PELARGONIUM)*
TYPE: HALF-HARDY ANNUAL (HHP TREATED AS HHA); NOT TO BE CONFUSED WITH THE HARDY GERANIUMS

Sowing time: Mid to late winter (very early spring at the latest), inside
Optimum temperature: 18–23°C (66–74°F)
Germination time: 3–21 days, but more rapid at 3–6 days, if given a constant temperature of 21–23°C (70–74°F)
Specific notes: Keep compost temperature and moisture constant for optimum germination, otherwise germination tends to occur in flushes. Grow seedlings on at 15°C (59°F)
Examples: 'Maverick Mixed' F1 hybrids 35–40cm (14–16in); 'Classic Scarlet' F1 30–38cm (12–15in); 'Summer Showers' F1 (cascading geranium) 30–45cm (12–18in). Flowering early summer until frosts

LEFT *Digitalis* 'Molten Ore'   ABOVE **A bicoloured geranium hybrid**

NAME: *HELIANTHUS* (SUNFLOWER)
TYPE: HARDY ANNUAL

Sowing time: Spring to early summer outside
Optimum temperature: 20°C (68°F), but will germinate at temperatures over 5°C (41°F)
Germination time: 10–21 days
Specific notes: Easy to grow, with varieties available from dwarf bedding types to giants. Sunflowers dislike being transplanted, so are best sown directly outside. They germinate best in warm soil, therefore sow late if possible. For a really early start, sow seed in peat pots inside in warmer temperatures and plant these out so that you don't disturb the roots. Seedlings grow rapidly, so start feeding as soon as they have germinated. If you want to collect your own seed, cover the developing seed-heads with netting to prevent birds eating the seeds. Only species will come true from your own seed, not hybrids
Examples: 'Velvet Queen' 1.5m (5ft) or more; 'Titan' 3.6m (12ft) with flower heads up to 60cm (24in) across; 'Pacino' 45cm (18in) – this is ideal for pots. Flowering takes place from mid-summer to mid-autumn

NAME: *HELICHRYSUM* (STRAW FLOWER)
TYPE: HARDY ANNUAL

Sowing time: Late winter to early spring inside, or spring outside
Optimum temperature: 18–20°C (66–68°F) inside, 10–12°C (50–54°F) outside
Germination time: 7–14 days
Specific notes: Best sown direct, or in modules in cold frame or cold greenhouse. Excellent for colour in borders and for use as dried flowers
Examples: *H. monstrosum* 'Bright Bikini Mixed' 38cm (15in) – a dwarf form; *H. monstrosum* Mixed 90–120cm (36–48in). Flowering early summer to early autumn

NAME: *IMPATIENS* (BUSY LIZZIE)
TYPE: HALF-HARDY ANNUAL (HHP TREATED AS HHA)

Sowing time: Late winter to mid-spring inside
Optimum temperature: 21–24°C (70–76°F)
Germination time: 10–21 days
Specific notes: Sow seeds on the surface of the compost as they require light – they can be covered very lightly with vermiculite. For best germination results, keep moist and humid by covering the seed tray with a layer of thin polythene, removing as soon as the seedlings start to emerge
Examples: 'Super Elfin' series of F1 hybrids, 25cm (10in), available in individual colours, for example 'Lipstick' (rose-pink), 'Salmon Blush' (peachy salmon) and 'Velvet Red' (deep red), or a mixture; 'Bruno' F1 hybrid, large tetraploid flowers up to 6cm (2.5in) across, growing to 23cm (9in). Flowering early summer until frosts

NAME: *LOBELIA*
TYPE: HALF-HARDY ANNUAL

Sowing time: Mid-winter to early spring inside
Optimum temperature: 18–21°C (66–70°F)
Germination time: 10–21 days
Specific notes: Sow thinly on the surface of moist compost and cover with clear polythene or a sheet of glass. Transplant or prick out clumps of several seedlings, as individually they are very tiny. This way you will get good-sized plants
Examples: *L. pendula* 'Cascade' (trailing lobelia); 'Cambridge Blue' 10cm (4in); 'Mrs Clibran Improved' 10cm (4in). Flowering early summer to mid-autumn

LEFT **A lemon-yellow sunflower (*Helianthus*)**

NAME: *PAPAVER* (POPPY)
TYPE: **HARDY ANNUAL**

Sowing time: Spring outside, or can be sown outside in early autumn for flowering the following year
Optimum temperature: 10–15°C (50–59°F)
Germination time: 7–30 days
Specific notes: Poppies really dislike being transplanted, so it is always preferable to sow them straight into the garden soil. Note that the seeds are harmful if eaten
Examples: *P. rhoeas* 'Angel Wings Mixed' 30cm (12in); *P. orientale* 'Princess Victoria Louise' 80cm (32in); *P. somniferum* 'Paeony Flowered Mixed' 90cm (36in); *P. paeoniflorum* 'Flemish Antique' 60–90cm (24–36in). Flowering late spring to late summer

NAME: *PETUNIA*
TYPE: **HALF-HARDY ANNUAL**

Sowing time: Late winter to mid-spring inside
Optimum temperature: 18–21°C (66–70°F)
Germination time: 7–14 days
Specific notes: Seeds are very tiny and the seedlings are slow growing, so you need to start early with petunias. Sow seed on the surface of the compost (do not cover), and keep moist and humid by covering the seed tray with clear polythene or a sheet of glass. Optimum germination occurs at constant warmth of at least 20°C (68°F). Remove the cover as soon as seedlings emerge. Maintain a temperature of 12–15°C (54–59°F) for seedling growth
Examples: 'Prism Mixed' F1 hybrids 30–35cm (12–14in); 'Mirage Midnight' F1 25–30cm

LEFT **French marigold 'Naughty Marietta'**

NAME: *TAGETES* (FRENCH MARIGOLD)
TYPE: HALF-HARDY ANNUAL

Sowing time: Late winter to mid-spring inside or late spring outside
Optimum temperature: 20°C (68°F)
Germination time: 3–7 days
Specific notes: Separate out the long seeds as much as possible and sow flat on compost, then cover. They germinate very rapidly, so don't sow too early in cold areas. Many are hybrids, so if you collect your own seed, the resulting plants will vary in colour and quality
Examples: 'Red Cherry' 25cm (10in); 'Naughty Marietta' 25cm (10in). Flowering early summer to mid-autumn

NAME: *VIOLA* (PANSY)
TYPE: HARDY OR HALF-HARDY ANNUAL
(HP NORMALLY GROWN AS HA/HHA)

Sowing time: This varies depending on the time of flowering, and you should follow the instructions on the seed packet. As a general guide, pansies that flower from spring to autumn should be sown from late winter to early spring inside. Pansies that flower from autumn to spring (known as 'winter pansies') are sown from early to mid-spring inside, or early to mid-summer in a cold frame
Optimum temperature: 15–18°C (59–66°F) for germination, then move immediately to a cooler temperature of 10–12°C (50–54°F) to keep seedlings compact
Germination time: 7–21 days
Specific notes: High temperatures can depress or prevent germination. Summer sowings especially must be kept cool, by keeping seed trays in a ventilated cold frame for example. Cover seed lightly with vermiculite and keep moist
Examples: 'Jolly Joker' F2 hybrid 20cm (8in) and 'Flambe' F1 hybrid 25cm (10in) (spring/autumn flowering); 'Ultima Morpho' F1 hybrid 15cm (6in) (autumn/spring flowering, very winter-hardy)

(10–12in); 'Polo Mixed' F1 25cm (10in). Flowering late spring to mid-autumn

NAME: *TAGETES* (AFRICAN MARIGOLD)
TYPE: HALF-HARDY ANNUAL

Sowing time: Late winter to mid-spring inside
Optimum temperature: 20–25°C (68–77°F)
Germination time: 4–14 days
Specific notes: Seeds are long and thin, so separate as much as possible and sow flat on compost before covering. Many are highly bred hybrids, so plants grown from seed saved yourself will vary in colour and quality
Examples: 'Inca Mixed' F1 hybrids, huge double flowers on very uniform compact plants, 25–30cm (9–12in); 'Sunspot Series' 20cm (8in). Flowering early summer to mid-autumn

ABOVE **A yellow-flowered Universal pansy**

MORE UNUSUAL ANNUALS AND BIENNIALS

NAME: *CERINTHE*
TYPE: **HARDY ANNUAL** (SHORT-LIVED HARDY
PERENNIAL IF SOWN IN AUTUMN)

Sowing time: Late winter to early spring inside
Optimum temperature: 18–20°C (66–68°F)
Germination time: 5–21 days
Specific notes: Don't sow too early as plants
grow rapidly and become tall and spindly if
you can't get them planted outside. They will
self-seed without any encouragement, and
seedlings will grow readily in the ground, often
forming stockier, stronger plants
Examples: C. *major purpurescens* 30–45cm
(12–18in); C. *minor aurea* 'Bouquet Gold'
35–45cm (14–18in). Flowering takes place
from late spring to mid-autumn

NAME: *GAZANIA*
TYPE: **HALF-HARDY ANNUAL**
(PERENNIAL TREATED AS HHA)

Sowing time: Late winter inside
Optimum temperature: 18–21°C (66–70°F)
Germination time: 14–21 days
Specific notes: Keep warm and do not
overwater at any stage – put outside only after
all danger of frost is gone. Brilliant jewel
colours for bedding or containers
Examples: 'Talent Series', bright flowers over

silvery-white foliage, 20cm (8in); 'Kiss Series', compact, free-flowering F1 hybrid, 20cm (8in). Flowering mid-summer to early autumn

NAME: *MESEMBRYANTHEMUM (LIVINGSTONE DAISY)*
TYPE: HALF-HARDY ANNUAL

Sowing time: Late winter to early spring
Optimum temperature: 15–20°C (59–68°F)
Germination time: 7–21 days
Specific notes: Lightly cover seeds with compost. Grow seedlings on at 10–12°C

(50–54°F) and do not overwater. Keep fairly dry once growing strongly in order to maximise flowering. Flowers open in sun, forming carpets of colour
Example: 'Magic Carpet Mixed' 8cm (3in). Flowering early summer to early autumn

BELOW **The striking flowers and bracts of** *Cerinthe major purpurescens*

NAME: *NEMOPHILA* (BABY BLUE EYES)
TYPE: **HARDY ANNUAL**

Sowing time: Spring
Optimum temperature: 18°C (66°F)
Germination time: 14–21 days
Specific notes: Rewarding to grow your own to fill baskets or containers for a mass of flowers on trailing plants
Examples: *Nemophila maculata* 'Pennie Black', rich purple, white edge, 10cm (4in); *N. maculata* 'Five Spot', white blue-tipped petals, 8–15cm (3–6in). Flowering early summer to early autumn

NAME: *PAPAVER NUDICAULE* (ICELAND POPPY)
TYPE: **HARDY BIENNIAL**

Sowing time: Mid-spring inside or mid-spring to early summer outside
Optimum temperature: 15–20°C (59–68°F)
Germination time: 7–21 days
Specific notes: Although it is best to sow in situ outside, as they dislike transplanting, the seed can be sown inside in Jiffy pots or deep cell trays to minimize root disturbance when planted out
Example: *P. nudicaule* 'Meadow Pastels', 60–70cm (24–32in). Flowering late spring to late summer

NAME: *PERILLA*
TYPE: **HALF-HARDY ANNUAL**

Sowing time: Late winter to mid-spring
Optimum temperature: 18–21°C (66–70°F)
Germination time: 14–21 days
Specific notes: Seeds require light, so leave uncovered or cover very lightly with vermiculite. They can be slow to germinate and may be erratic. Excellent bedding or accent plant
Example: *P. frutescens nankinensis*, has attractive deep purple-red foliage, deeply cut and crinkled, 60cm (24in). Flowering mid-winter to late spring

NAME: *PORTULACA*
TYPE: **HALF-HARDY ANNUAL**

Sowing time: Late winter to early spring inside
Optimum temperature: 21–24°C (70–76°F)
Germination time: 7–10 days
Specific notes: Sow seeds on surface of compost and keep moist, covering tray with clear polythene or a sheet of glass. Prick out clumps of seedlings rather than individuals. Lovely small plants for hot sunny positions and containers
Examples: *P. grandiflora* 'Sundial Mixed', large, bright flowers, F1 hybrid, 20cm (8in); *P. grandiflora* 'Kariba Mixed', large double flowers, F2, 10–15cm (4–6in). Flowering early summer onwards

NAME: *RUDBECKIA* (CONE FLOWER)
TYPE: **HALF-HARDY ANNUAL** (NOTE THERE ARE ALSO PERENNIAL RUDBECKIAS)

Sowing time: Late winter to mid-spring inside or mid to late spring outside
Optimum temperature: 18–20°C (66–68°F)
Germination time: 7–21 days
Specific notes: Excellent easy-to-grow bedding plants with a colour range of yellow, gold, bronze and orange
Examples: Forms of *Rudbeckia hirta* include 'Marmalade' 45cm (18in); 'Rustic Dwarfs' 60cm (24in); 'Green Eyes' 45cm (18in). Flowering mid-summer to mid-autumn

NAME: *VERBENA*
TYPE: **HALF-HARDY ANNUAL**

Sowing time: Mid-winter to early spring inside
Optimum temperature: 18–25°C (66–77°F)
Germination time: 14–21 days
Specific notes: Seeds germinate best in the dark. When sowing, cover seeds with almost dry compost as they are sensitive to too much moisture, and place seed tray in total darkness. Inspect regularly and move to light conditions once germination has occurred. Some varieties, including the popular 'Peaches

& Cream', can have lower germination rates
Examples: *Verbena* x *hybrida* 'Romance Pastels Mixed' 15cm (6in); *V.* x *hybrida* 'Peaches & Cream' 23cm (9in). These plants flower from early summer to mid-autumn

NAME: *ZINNIA*
TYPE: **HALF-HARDY ANNUAL**

Sowing time: Early to mid-spring inside or late spring to early summer outside
Optimum temperature: 20°C (68°F) for inside germination; only sow outside in the garden once soil has warmed up
Germination time: 7–10 days

ABOVE Flowers of *Rudbeckia* are usually in autumnal shades

Specific notes: Best sown in situ as it resents root disturbance. Alternatively, sow in peat pots or directly into plastic pots inside, germinate at 20°C (68°F) then grow seedlings on at lower temperature of 15–18°C (59–66°F)
Examples: *Z. elegans* 'Dreamland Red', F1 hybrid, 25cm (10in); *Z. elegans* 'Candy Cane', double flecked flowers, 60cm (24in); *Z. haageana* 'Persian Carpet', double bicolour flowers, 30cm (12in). Zinnias flower from mid-summer to mid-autumn

CHAPTER 6

Perennials from seed

WHAT ARE PERENNIALS?

A perennial is a plant that lives for two or more years, is non-woody and usually herbaceous, dying back to soil level in late autumn. New growth emerges in spring, and the majority of perennials produce their flower display in summer and early autumn. There are a number, however, that flower in spring or in autumn and winter. Some perennials are evergreen, retaining their foliage above ground all year round.

All the perennials discussed in this chapter are hardy, meaning that they can withstand a certain amount of frost.

It is rewarding to grow perennials from seed, particularly if you want a number of the same plant to form a group. While some perennials will flower the same year from an early sowing, many will produce foliage and establish themselves the first year before starting to flower in their second year.

USES IN THE GARDEN

Perennials are available in a huge range of sizes, shapes and colours, with great diversity in foliage and flower, and they are on the whole extremely reliable and long-lived. You can use them to create herbaceous borders or grow them in mixed borders among shrubs, climbers and annuals, or even in containers.

Herbaceous borders on any scale look better with groups of plants, creating blocks or drifts of colour rather than single specimens of each. Place contrasting foliage types together, and arrange them so that the flower colours don't clash. Try different colour schemes, such as soft pinks and lilac with cream or white; or blue, yellow and gold. Hot colours such as strong yellow, orange, red and mahogany give strong impact.

Use perennials in mixed borders to continue the floral display after spring bulbs and early summer shrubs have finished. This provides more year-round interest to borders, especially if you use both evergreen and deciduous shrubs. Large perennials can be planted singly, but smaller ones are still better in groups of three or more.

The main season for massed colour with perennials is summer and early autumn, and most will require cutting back as their foliage starts to die down. However, some perennials have attractive seed-heads that are worth leaving, for the structural effect as well as autumn colour.

GROWING REQUIREMENTS

Perennials can often be sown directly outside in spring, which is particularly useful if you intend growing a group or large patch of the same variety. Prepare the ground thoroughly and keep it watered once the seed has been sown. Remove weed seedlings promptly, and thin out the perennial seedlings to the required spacing.

ABOVE **The dramatic flowers of** *Aquilegia vulgaris* **'William Guiness'**

Most perennials are best sown in pans or trays, then you can select the strongest ones to grow on. You are likely to require less of each variety than is the case with annuals. This also gives you the opportunity to sow early in the season, pot the seedlings up, grow them on, and plant them out exactly where you want them. Many perennials will also flower in their first year with this method of growing.

As detailed in the individual plants that follow, some perennial seeds will not germinate until they have been exposed to a period of cold. This can be achieved by sowing the seed in a pan or tray and leaving them in a sheltered spot outside, or by placing them in a ventilated cold frame. Others germinate either more readily or more slowly, or over an extended period, in a heated propagator. If you buy seed from a commercial supplier, take note of the instructions on the packet.

Freshly collected seeds are always worth sowing immediately, particularly those of plants such as *Helleborus*, *Cyclamen* and *Pulsatilla*, as they very often germinate rapidly before inhibitors or dormancy set in. If you purchase seeds such as these, sow as soon as possible and leave them in a cold frame, or outside – don't store them any longer than is necessary.

POPULAR PERENNIALS

From pages 76 to 91 we have listed some of the perennial plants commonly grown in gardens, with details of sowing and some specific requirements. We have suggested two or three named species or hybrids, or seed mixtures available from commercial seed suppliers. Many of the seed firms' catalogues have pictures of the plants, so it is worth looking through them to make your own choice.

LEFT *Coreopsis grandiflora* 'Early Sunrise' produces golden blooms for many weeks

NAME: *ACHILLEA* (YARROW)
TYPE: **HARDY PERENNIAL**

Sowing time: Late winter to early summer inside

Optimum temperature: 20°C (68°F)

Germination time: 7–14 days

Specific notes: Germination is generally rapid. Surface sow. Cover the seeds lightly and keep them moist, in a warm temperature. These are easy-going border plants, and are excellent for cut flowers and for drying

Examples: *A. ptarmica* 'The Pearl', white button-like flowers in loose sprays, 60cm (24in); *A. filipendula* 'Cloth of Gold', large, flat, deep yellow heads, 120cm (48in); *A. millefolium* 'Cerise Queen', range of pinks and reds, 60cm (24in). Flowering summer

NAME: *ANTHEMIS* (GOLDEN MARGUERITE)
TYPE: **HARDY PERENNIAL**

Sowing time: Mid-winter to early spring inside, or late spring to early summer outside

Optimum temperature: 18–20°C (66–68°F)

Germination time: 14–30 days

Specific needs: Cover seed thinly and keep at a constant temperature. Ideal plants for the border, they are also excellent cut flowers

Examples: *A. tinctoria* 'Kelwayi', lemon yellow, 40–60cm (16–24in); *A. sancti-johannis*, bright orange, 40cm (16in). Flowering takes place from mid-summer to mid-autumn

RIGHT *Helleborus orientalis* hybrid

NAME: *AQUILEGIA* (COLUMBINE)
TYPE: HARDY PERENNIAL

Sowing time: Seeds germinate best if sown fresh (summer); purchased seed sown in mid-winter to early spring may require pre-chilling as below

Optimum temperature: 15–20°C (59–68°F). Stored seeds may need a cold period of 4–6 weeks outside or in a refrigerator, which should improve the germination rate

Germination time: 7–14 days when freshly sown, otherwise may be 30–90 days

Specific notes: Some species may require a cold period. After the chilling period, germination may take a long time, so keep the seed trays at least until the following year. Seeds need light for germination so do not cover. Aquilegias cross-pollinate readily, so it is difficult to produce your own seed that will come true, unless plants are isolated from other species. However, they self-sow easily, and all kinds of interesting crosses can be achieved. Note: seeds and plants may be harmful if eaten

Examples: *A. vulgaris* 'William Guiness', dramatic deep purple, almost black, and white, 60cm (24in); *A.* x *hybrida* 'McKana Giants Mixed', clear bright flowers, reliable, 75–90cm (30–36in); *A. flabellata*, blue and cream, 23–30cm (9–12in). Flowering late spring to mid-summer

NAME: *CAMPANULA* (BELLFLOWER)
TYPE: HARDY PERENNIAL

Sowing time: Early spring to early summer for planting out in autumn. If you collect your own seed (only species will come true), sow fresh when it should germinate readily, and plants can then be put outside in spring

Optimum temperature: 10–15°C (50–59°F), best germinated in a cold frame

LEFT **A pink-flowered plant of** *Lobelia speciosa* **'Fan Series Mixed'**

ABOVE *Lychnis coronaria* has magenta blooms and felted silvery foliage

Germination time: 7–14 days, but may take up to 90 days

Specific notes: Some species may need pre-chilling. The seeds are very tiny and need light, so cover only sparingly or just press into compost surface, and make sure the compost does not dry out, particularly where trays are being kept for a long period. Keep lightly shaded, or at least out of direct sunlight

Examples: Range from dwarf to very tall types. *Campanula carpatica* 'Blue & White Uniform' is an F1 hybrid, a compact form with upturned blue or white flowers, 15–20cm (6–8in); *C. takesimana*, creamy bells spotted maroon inside, 45–60cm (18–24in); *C. lactiflora* 'Mixed Colours', blue, pink or white starry flowers on long stems, good cut flower, up to 1.5m (5ft). All flower in summer

ABOVE **A deep purple flower of** *Platycodon grandiflorum*

NAME: *COREOPSIS*
TYPE: **HARDY PERENNIAL**
(THERE ARE ALSO ANNUAL COREOPSIS)

Sowing time: Mid-winter to mid-spring inside, or mid-spring to early summer outside
Optimum temperature: 18–22°C (66–72°F)
Germination time: 7–14 days
Specific notes: Seeds need light for germination, so press gently into compost surface or cover very lightly with vermiculite. Perennial coreopsis will flower in their first year from an early sowing. Dead-head regularly to prolong the display. They make good cut flowers
Examples: *C. grandiflora* 'Early Sunrise', bright golden yellow, semi-double, 45cm (18in); *C. rosea* 'American Dream', pink flowers, delicate green foliage, 60cm (24in). Flowering early summer to mid-autumn

NAME: *DELPHINIUM*
TYPE: **HARDY PERENNIAL**

Sowing time: Late winter to mid-spring inside, late spring to mid-summer outside
Optimum temperature: 15–18°C (59–66°F)
Germination time: 15–40 days
Specific notes: For best germination results, maintain constant humidity, by covering tray with a layer of thin polythene, or with a clear propagator lid. Note: seeds are toxic if eaten. Flowers are attractive to bees and butterflies, and can be used for cutting
Examples: *Delphinium hybrida* 'Magic Fountains Mixed', good spikes in white and shades of blue and lilac, 75–90cm (30–36in); *D. hybrida* 'Pacific Giants Mixed', traditional mixture, 1.2–1.5m (4–5ft). All forms flower from early to mid-summer

NAME: *ERYNGIUM* (SEA HOLLY)
TYPE: **HARDY PERENNIAL**

Sowing time: Late autumn to early spring
Optimum temperature: 10–15°C (50–59°F), best germinated in a cold frame
Germination time: 100–130 days
Specific notes: Sow fresh seed in spring after winter chilling, or they will need a pre-chilling period before moving to a warmer temperature. Sow on surface of compost; cover with grit
Examples: *E. alpinum superbum*, dark blue flowers, deeply toothed glossy foliage, 60cm 24in); *E. variifolium*, striking marbled spiky foliage, silvery blue flowers, 38cm (15in); *E. giganteum* 'Miss Wilmott's Ghost', decorative steel-blue flowers surrounded by silvery bracts – a short-lived perennial, but usually self-seeds well, 90cm (36in). Flowering early summer to early autumn

NAME: *EUPHORBIA* (SPURGE)
TYPE: **HARDY PERENNIAL**

Sowing time: Late autumn to mid-spring
Optimum temperature: 10–12°C (50–54°F), best germinated in a cold frame
Germination time: 21 days to 12 months
Specific notes: Seeds germinate irregularly over a long period, so don't discard seed trays for at least a year. Note: seeds are harmful if eaten, and the sap of the plants can cause irritation, so wear gloves when handling
Examples: *E. characias* subsp. *wulfenii*, huge heads of lime-green, 60–90cm (24–36in); *E. mellifera*, golden heads with honey fragrance, 60cm (24in); *E. myrsinites*, trailing with greenish-yellow flowers, 15–23cm (6–10in)

BELOW **The rounded flower head of the drumstick primula,** *Primula denticulata*

ABOVE *Pulsatilla vulgaris* 'Eva Constance' – a red form that comes largely true from seed

NAME: *GAURA*
TYPE: HARDY PERENNIAL

Sowing time: Spring under glass or early summer outside

Optimum temperature: 18–20°C (66–68°F) under glass

Germination time: 21–60 days

Specific notes: Long-flowering elegant perennial that flowers in its first year from seed if sown early in the season

Example: *G. lindheimeri* 'The Bride', long spikes of white flowers tinged pink, 90–120cm (36–48in). Flowering period is from mid-summer to mid-autumn

LEFT *Veronica spicata* 'Blue Bouquet' will usually flower the first year from sowing

NAME: *HELLEBORUS* (HELLEBORE)
TYPE: HARDY PERENNIAL

Sowing time: Autumn, or as soon as ripe if you collect your own seed

Optimum temperature: 5–10°C (41–50°F), best sown in a cold frame

Germination time: 30 days up to 18 months

Specific notes: Seeds require a cold period. Sow thinly as soon as ripe or available, and cover with grit. Leave seed containers outside or in a well-ventilated cold frame; bring under cover once germination starts. Keep in a cold frame or cold greenhouse and pot up seedlings individually into small pots when large enough to handle. Note: seeds are harmful if eaten

Examples: *H. orientalis* hybrids, maroon or pink flowers, some spotted, early winter to mid-spring, 45cm (18in); *H. sternii*, creamy green flowers from mid-winter to late spring, 35–45cm (14–18in)

83

NAME: *HEUCHERA* (CORAL BELLS)
TYPE: HARDY PERENNIAL

Sowing time: Early to mid-spring
Optimum temperature: 20–25°C (68–77°F).
To break germination inhibitors of stored seeds, keep at 25°C (77°F) for six weeks, then place in a cold frame for germination to begin
Germination time: 10–60 days
Specific notes: Seed germinates slowly and irregularly over a long period. The seeds are very tiny, so just press gently into surface of compost, and do not allow them to dry out
Examples: *H. americana* 'Palace Purple', bronze leaves, white flowers, 60cm (24in); *H. pulchella*, pale pink, 30–45cm (12–18in). Flowers early summer to early autumn

NAME: *LOBELIA*
TYPE: HARDY PERENNIAL

Sowing time: Late winter to mid-spring inside
Optimum temperature: 20–25°C (68–77°F)
Germination time: 14–30 days
Specific notes: Seeds generally germinate readily. *L. speciosa* types germinate better at the higher temperature, with constant humidity. Seeds are very tiny, so just press gently into surface of the compost and do not cover. Takes one to two years to flower from sowing
Examples: *L. cardinalis*, scarlet flowers, maroon leaves, 90cm (36in); *L. speciosa* 'Fan Series Mixed' F1 hybrid, green or bronzed foliage, flowers rose pink, red and purple, 60cm (24in). Flowering late summer to mid-autumn

NAME: *LUPINUS* (LUPIN)
TYPE: HARDY PERENNIAL

Sowing time: Mid to late winter inside for planting late spring for same-year flowering; or mid-spring to early summer outside for flowering the following year

LEFT *Asphodelus albus*, a striking perennial to grow from seed

Optimum temperature: 15–18°C (59–66°F) under glass
Germination time: 14–21 days
Specific notes: Soak or chip seed to soften or break the hard seed-coat. Cover with a layer of compost. Note: seeds are harmful if eaten
Examples: *L. regalis* 'Band of Nobles Mixed', bright colours, 90–120cm (36–48in); *L. regalis* 'Dwarf Gallery Mixed', dwarf, bicoloured flowers, 23–50cm (9–20in). Flowering late spring to mid-summer

NAME: *LYCHNIS* (CAMPION)
TYPE: HARDY PERENNIAL

Sowing time: Late winter under glass or late spring outside
Optimum temperature: 15–20°C (59–68°F) under glass
Germination time: 14–30 days
Specific notes: If after 30 days there are no signs of germination, pre-chill for 14–30 days before moving back to a warmer temperature
Examples: *L. arkwrightii* 'Vesuvius', bronzed maroon foliage, vivid orange-red flowers, does not flower until second year, 45cm (18in); *L. chalcedonica*, scarlet flowers, 90cm (36in). Flowering early summer to early autumn

NAME: *OENOTHERA* (EVENING PRIMROSE)
TYPE: HARDY PERENNIAL

Sowing time: Mid-winter to early spring inside or mid-spring to early summer in trays or modules in a cold frame
Optimum temperature: 20°C (68°F)
Germination time: 14–30 days
Specific notes: Flowers appear in the first season if seed is sown early
Examples: *Oenothera speciosa* 'Pink Petticoats', soft pink, fragrant, 40cm (16in); *O. odorata* 'Apricot Delight', lemon yellow maturing to apricot then salmon pink, 60cm (24in). Flowering late spring to late summer depending on variety

NAME: *PLATYCODON (BALLOON FLOWER)*
TYPE: **HARDY PERENNIAL**

Sowing time: Mid-winter to early spring inside, or late spring to early summer outside
Optimum temperature: 20°C (68°F)
Germination time: 10–30 days
Specific notes: Seeds require light for germination, so just press gently into surface of compost. The seedlings dislike being transplanted, so place seed in individual small pots or modules to avoid disturbing the roots. Handle seedlings carefully, as they are quite fragile. Seeds can also be sown directly outside, once all danger of frost is past
Examples: *Platycodon grandiflorum* 'Fairy Snow', white flowers veined blue, 25cm (10in); *P. grandiflorum* 'Mariesii', deep blue, 50cm (20in). Flowering summer

NAME: *PRIMULA*
TYPE: **HARDY PERENNIAL**
(THERE ARE HARDY SPECIES AND HYBRIDS, AS WELL AS POLYANTHUS AND PRIMROSE HYBRIDS)

Sowing time: Most hardy forms – mid-winter inside, spring outside; Polyanthus – spring inside; Primrose – mid-winter to early summer inside. If you collect your own seed, sow as soon as ripe in summer in a cold frame
Optimum temperature: 15–18°C (59–66°F)
Germination time: 10–30 days
Specific notes: Sow on surface of compost, keep moist and cool. Primulas have been known to cause skin irritation
Examples: Polyanthus – 'Gold Lace', deep crimson laced gold, 20cm (8in); 'Heritage Mixed', very winter-hardy, fragrant, 25cm (10in). Primrose – 'Wanda Supreme Mixed', dark bronze-green leaves, vibrant-coloured, yellow-eyed flowers, 10–15cm (4–6in).

Hardy forms – *Primula denticulata*, the drumstick primula, ball-shaped heads of white or mauve, 23–30cm (9–12in); *Primula vialii*, spikes of crimson and violet, 30cm (12in). Flowering spring

NAME: *PULSATILLA (PASQUE FLOWER)*
TYPE: **HARDY PERENNIAL**

Sowing time: Mid-autumn to late winter outside, early spring inside
Optimum temperature: 10–12°C (50–54°F) in a cold frame; 18–20°C (66–68°F) inside
Germination time: 30 days to 9 months
Specific notes: Fresh seed sown immediately usually germinates readily, and established plants will self-seed. Stored or purchased seed needs a cold period for 4–6 weeks – keep in a cold frame. Seedlings are slow to develop
Examples: *P. vulgaris*, violet and mauve shades, 20cm (8in); *P. alpina* 'Sulphurea', sulphur-yellow, 25cm (10in). Flowering spring

NAME: *SCABIOSA (SCABIOUS)*
TYPE: **HARDY PERENNIAL**

Sowing time: Spring
Optimum temperature: 18–21°C (66–70°F)
Germination time: 7–40 days
Specific notes: For best germination results *Scabiosa caucasica* and its cultivars need a temperature of 21°C (70°F) and constant humidity. Other species tend to germinate irregularly over a long period, and are better kept at a lower temperature
Examples: *S. caucasica* 'Fama', deep lavender flowers, ideal for cutting, 50cm (20in); *S. graminifolia*, pale lilac, 35cm (14in). Flowering early summer to early autumn

LEFT **The marbled leaves of *Cyclamen hederifolium* in autumn**

NAME: *VERONICA* (SPEEDWELL)
TYPE: **HARDY PERENNIAL**

Sowing time: Mid-winter to early spring inside, or mid-spring to early summer outside or in a cold frame
Optimum temperature: 15–20°C (59–68°F)
Germination time: 20–30 days
Specific notes: Seeds germinate readily and rapidly. Cover seed thinly, or just press into compost surface if very small. Keep seedlings at a lower temperature once germinated
Examples: *V. gentianoides*, very pale blue spikes, 45–60cm (18–24in); *V. spicata* 'Blue Bouquet', flowers first year from seed, intense blue spikes, 30–45cm (12–18in); *V. longifolia*, 'Rose Tones', rosy pink, 90cm (36in). Flowering summer

MORE UNUSUAL PERENNIALS

NAME: *AGASTACHE* (MEXICAN HYSSOP)
TYPE: **HARDY PERENNIAL**

Sowing time: Late winter to early spring inside, or late spring to early summer outside
Optimum temperature: 15–22°C (59–72°F)
Germination time: 7–30 days
Specific notes: Germination is generally easy and rapid, though may be irregular. Cover seed thinly. Flower spikes are attractive to bees and butterflies
Examples: *A. foeniculum*, aniseed-scented foliage, mauve-blue flowers, 90cm (36in); *A. aurantiaca* 'Apricot Sprite', 38–45cm (15–18in). Flowering takes place from mid-summer to mid-autumn

NAME: *ASPHODELUS*
TYPE: **HARDY PERENNIAL**

Sowing time: Mid-winter to early summer
Optimum temperature: 15–20°C (59–68°F)
Germination time: 30–90 days
Specific notes: Grows readily from seed, producing tufts of long slender leaves and decorative spikes of white, starry flowers
Examples: *A. albus* 90cm (36in); *A. ramosus* 1.2m (4ft). Flowering late spring to summer

RIGHT **Seed-heads of *Cyclamen hederifolium***

NAME: *ASTRANTIA*
TYPE: HARDY PERENNIAL

Sowing time: Mid-winter to early spring inside, or autumn outside
Optimum temperature: 10–15°C (50–59°F)
Germination time: 30–180 days
Specific notes: Seeds need a cold period of up to six weeks, so keep seed tray outside or in a well-ventilated cold frame. Excellent for moisture-retentive soils, good cut flowers
Examples: *A. major*, silvery pink, 60–90cm (24–36in); *A. major* 'Ruby Cloud', ruby red

tinged green, 75cm (30in); *A. major* 'Sunningdale Variegated', leaves splashed yellow and cream, pinkish-green flowers – seedlings will need selecting for those with variegated foliage, discarding plain green ones, 60–75cm (24–30in). Flowering summer

NAME: *CYCLAMEN*
TYPE: HARDY PERENNIAL

Sowing time: Mid-autumn to early spring
Optimum temperature: Best sown in a cold frame in a temperature of 10°C (50°F)
Germination time: 30 days – 12 months
Specific notes: Sow collected seeds as soon as ripe – these should germinate readily. Soak stored seeds in tepid water for 24 hours prior to sowing to soften the seed-coat. Space seeds out and cover with grit. Leave seedlings of hardy cyclamen two years before potting individually, allowing the tubers time to develop. Seed will germinate at the time the plants normally emerge (late summer and autumn), the seedlings dying down over spring. When they emerge again, they can be potted up. Most cyclamen species take three years to flower from seed. Once planted out, they will self-seed to form colonies, particularly attractive beneath trees or shrubs
Examples: *C. coum*, carmine or white flowers in winter, 10cm (4in); *C. hederifolium*, pink flowers in autumn, marbled leaves, 15cm (6in)

NAME: *ERODIUM*
TYPE: HARDY PERENNIAL

Sowing time: Late winter to mid-spring inside
Optimum temperature: 12–21°C (54–70°F)
Germination time: 20–36 days
Specific notes: Germination may be slow and can often be irregular
Examples: *E. pelargoniiflorum*, white, pink-veined flowers resembling a small geranium, 20–30cm (8–12in); *E. manescaui*, magenta flowers, self-seeds prolifically, 40cm (16in). Flowering late spring to autumn

NAME: *GENTIANA (GENTIAN)*
TYPE: **HARDY PERENNIAL**

Sowing time: Late summer to early winter outside or in a cold frame
Optimum temperature: 8–10°C (41–50°F)
Germination time: 80–120 days
Specific notes: Many require a cold period of three to six weeks before germination will occur. Even with this treatment, germination may be erratic, so don't discard seed trays too soon. Sow freshly collected seed immediately. Note that different blue shades will be produced among seed-raised plants
Examples: *G. asclepiadea*, deep blue flowers, for damp shady spot, 45cm (18in); *G. acaulis*, deep blue trumpet flowers, 10cm (4in)

NAME: *HELENIUM*
TYPE: **HARDY PERENNIAL**

Sowing time: Late winter to mid-spring inside, or late spring to mid-summer outside
Optimum temperature: 18°C (66°F) inside
Germination time: 20–30 days
Specific notes: Although helenium seeds generally germinate easily and rapidly, they may be erratic
Examples: *H. autumnale* 'Sunshine Hybrid', dark-centred flowers of yellow, gold, orange, red and mahogany, 60–120cm (24–48in); *H. autumnale* 'Autumn Leaves', vibrant shades of yellow, gold and red, each with a dark centre. 1.2m (4ft). Flowering takes place early summer to mid-autumn

NAME: *IRIS*
TYPE: **HARDY PERENNIAL**

Sowing time: Autumn
Optimum temperature: 5–15°C (41–59°F), best sown in a cold frame
Germination time: 30 days – 18 months
Specific notes: Seeds are best sown when fresh. Soak seeds to soften the hard outer coat. After sowing, place the seed tray outside in the shade, as a cold period is required for successful germination. Flowering takes two to four years
Examples: *I. chrysographes* 'Black Knight', deep purple-black flowers, variable from seed, 45–60cm (18–24in); *I.* 'Pacific Coast Hybrids', range of colours, 45cm (18in)

NAME: *SCUTELLARIA*
TYPE: **HARDY PERENNIAL**

Sowing time: Late winter to early spring inside
Optimum temperature: 18–20°C (66–68°F)
Germination time: 21–60 days
Specific notes: Generally germinate rapidly and easily. Pretty, long-flowering small plants for rock garden or front of well-drained border. Self-seed readily
Examples: *S. baicalensis*, purple-blue flowers, 30cm (12in); *S. orientalis*, bright yellow flowers, 20cm (8in). Flowering summer

NAME: *STACHYS*
TYPE: **HARDY PERENNIAL**

Sowing time: Mid-spring to early summer
Optimum temperature: 15–18°C (59–66°F)
Germination time: 30–90 days
Specific notes: Seeds may germinate irregularly over a long period, so do not discard seed trays too early
Examples: *S. byzantina*, silver velvety leaves, lilac flowers, 30cm (12in); *S. monieri* carries green leaves and pink flowers, 30cm (12in)

LEFT *Iris suaveolens*, a miniature iris

CHAPTER 7

Trees and shrubs from seed

WHAT ARE TREES AND SHRUBS?

Trees and shrubs provide the woody permanent framework in a garden. They tend to be slow growing, often taking many years to reach a significant size and as such are not the most obvious subjects to grow from seed. However, many are not difficult to grow from seed, and it is very satisfying to see a tree you have nurtured from a small seed develop over several years.

Many popular ornamental trees are selected hybrids, and while most of these will produce viable seeds these will very rarely come true to type, instead producing a very varied crop of seedlings. Hybrids need to be propagated vegetatively (by means of cuttings, layering, division, and so on) to ensure they remain true to type. Trees and shrubs that are pure species will usually come true from seed and this can be the best method of propagation for many of them.

GROWING REQUIREMENTS

For successful results with trees and shrubs, fresh seed is very important. This is often the reason why seed from retail seed merchants fails to germinate. Large seeds such as *Quercus* and *Aesculus* will not germinate if they are allowed to dry out and should be sown as soon as possible for good results. Many smaller seeds will also gradually lose their ability to germinate as they begin to dry out.

Most trees and shrubs will flower and produce fruit by late summer or autumn. Seeds collected at this time are best sown immediately into pots of compost and then left over winter in a cold frame where they are exposed to the normal seasonal fluctuations of temperature. We have found that with many common trees and shrubs this can be just as effective as trying to recreate the same conditions in a refrigerator (low temperature) or airing cupboard (warm temperature). Seeds of species such as *Lavandula* and *Cistus*, which originate in temperate areas, are best stored in cool conditions over winter and then sown into pots in a greenhouse or cold frame in spring.

Germination times for many woody plants are much longer than for annuals, and patience is required. Seeds sown in the autumn may well not germinate until late spring or even, in some cases, the following spring. Because of this it is important to top-dress the containers with grit, which will help to prevent the build-up of moss and liverworts. Ensure also that only clean water is used (see chapter 4). The large seeds of many woody plants are natural food for some small mammals, so it is important to exclude them wherever possible, and the seeds should be protected from rodents by means of traps.

Small seeds, such as *Betula* or *Acer palmatum*, can be sown into pans or deep trays, but large seeds, such as *Quercus* or *Castanea*, are best

RIGHT **The seeds of *Aesculus hippocastanum* are the familiar shiny chestnuts or 'conkers'**

sown into individual pots. The seedlings of many woody plants will grow away rapidly once they have germinated, and they should be potted on regularly to prevent any checks to growth. Although they have many years of growth ahead of them the first few months are critical – if they become restricted at this stage they may never recover sufficiently to develop into strong specimens.

POPULAR TREES AND SHRUBS

NAME: *AESCULUS*
TYPE: **DECIDUOUS TREE**

Sowing time: Autumn
Optimum temperature: 5–10°C (41–50°F)
Germination time: 4–5 months
Specific notes: The seed will not germinate if it dries out so sow in the autumn, as soon after collection as possible. The seed must be ripe (a good brown colour) before collecting; in poor summers the seed may not ripen fully. Sow the seeds in individual deep pots, then pot on or plant out the seedlings before the tap root begins to spiral in the pot
Examples: *Aesculus hippocastanum* (horse chestnut); *Aesculus* x *carnea* (although this is a hybrid it usually comes fairly true from seed)

NAME: *BERBERIS* (BARBERRY)
TYPE: **DECIDUOUS AND EVERGREEN SHRUBS**

Sowing time: Spring
Optimum temperature: Needs cold period
Germination time: 4–5 months
Specific notes: Harvest berries in the autumn and store mixed with sand in containers. From late winter inspect the containers regularly and when the first signs of germination are seen sow the seed and sand together into pots or deep trays of compost, covering with a thin layer of grit. Only the species will come true from seed
Examples: *Berberis darwinii* (evergreen); *Berberis thunbergii* (deciduous).

LEFT **Berries of *Cotoneaster***

ABOVE Rich red berries of hawthorn, *Crataegus monogyna*

NAME: *BETULA (BIRCH)*
TYPE: **DECIDUOUS TREE**

Sowing time: Autumn or early spring
Optimum temperature: 5–10°C (41–50°F)
Germination time: Autumn-sown 4–5 months; spring-sown 3–4 weeks
Specific notes: Birch seeds can be stored in cooled conditions for several months without significant loss of germination. Birches are very promiscuous and cross-species hybridization occurs readily, resulting in a very variable crop of seedlings. If true species are required, you should collect seed from isolated trees, or propagate vegetatively
Examples: *Betula pendula* (silver birch); *Betula ermanii*; *Betula albo-sinensis*

NAME: *CISTUS (SUN ROSE)*
TYPE: **EVERGREEN SHRUB**

Sowing time: Mid to late spring
Optimum temperature: 10–15°C (50–59°F)
Germination time: 2–4 weeks
Specific notes: Sow the seed thinly as the small seeds produce robust seedlings, which can quickly become overcrowded. Pot on seedlings as soon as they are large enough to handle. Hybrid varieties will not come true
Examples: *Cistus laurifolius*; *Cistus albidus*

NAME: *COTONEASTER*
TYPE: **EVERGREEN AND DECIDUOUS SHRUBS**

Sowing time: Autumn
Optimum temperature: Needs cold period
Germination time: 4–5 months
Specific notes: Collect the berries as soon as they are ripe in the autumn. Separate the seeds from the flesh by crushing and then washing through a coarse sieve. Sow into deep pans in a cold frame. The species hybridizes readily and seeds should be collected from isolated plants to be sure of coming true
Examples: *Cotoneaster horizontalis*; *Cotoneaster lacteus*; *Cotoneaster frigidus*

ABOVE **The orange seeds and attractive pink outer coat of spindle,** *Euonymus europaeus*

NAME: *CRATAEGUS*
TYPE: **DECIDUOUS SHRUB/SMALL TREE**

Sowing time: Spring
Optimum temperature: The seed of this plant
needs to be stratified
Germination time: 18 months from collection;
4–12 weeks after sowing
Specific notes: The berries should be collected
as soon as they are ripe and the seed
extracted from the fleshy coats. The seeds can
then be placed in trays of damp sand or
vermiculite and left in a cold shed until the
second spring after collection. Sow the seed,
before it starts to germinate, into trays of
moistened compost
Examples: *Crataegus monogyna* (hawthorn);
Crataegus prunifolia

NAME: *CYTISUS* (BROOM)
TYPE: **EVERGREEN SHRUB**

Sowing time: Early spring
Optimum temperature: 10–15°C (50–59°F)
Germination time: 3–6 weeks
Specific needs: Soak seeds for 24 to 48
hours before sowing to soften the hard seed-
coat. Sow seeds into deep trays and prick out
into individual pots as soon as they are large
enough to handle. The plants should be
planted out before they reach about 30cm
(12in) as larger plants can be difficult to
establish. Hybrid forms, of course, will not
come true from seed
Examples: *Cytisus scoparius* (common broom);
Cytisus battandieri (Moroccan broom)

ABOVE **New spring growth on *Picea***

NAME: *EUCALYPTUS* (GUM TREE)
TYPE: **EVERGREEN TREE**

Sowing time: Late winter to early spring
Optimum temperature: 15–20°C (59–68°F)
Germination time: 8–10 weeks
Specific notes: Locally collected seed is ideal, as the seedlings should be better adapted to the local climate. Sow the seeds into individual deep pots in a warm greenhouse. The seedlings should be hardened off carefully before planting out. Do not allow the plants to become pot-bound as this has the effect of stunting subsequent root development, and can result in unstable trees
Examples: *Eucalyptus gunnii; Eucalyptus coccifera* and *Eucalyptus parvifolia*

NAME: *EUONYMUS* (DECIDUOUS VARIETIES)
TYPE: **DECIDUOUS SHRUBS**

Sowing time: Autumn
Optimum temperature: Needs cold period
Germination time: 4–5 months
Specific notes: Collect the seed capsules as they begin to split, and leave them in a tray covered with a sheet of paper until they have split and shed the seeds. The fleshy orange coat can then be removed carefully, before sowing the seeds into pots of compost in a cold frame. The seedlings should be pricked out as soon as they are large enough to handle, taking care not to damage the tender stem and brittle roots
Examples: *Euonymus europaeus* (spindle); *Euonymus alatus*

ABOVE **Seedlings of** *Pinus pumila*

NAME: *FAGUS* (BEECH)
TYPE: **DECIDUOUS TREE**

Sowing time: Autumn
Optimum temperature: Needs a cold period
before germination
Germination time: 4–5 months
Specific notes: Beech seeds should be
collected as soon as they fall in autumn, and
then sown immediately. The seed is very
attractive to rodents and should be protected
until germination. Beech is susceptible to root
damage and seedlings should be potted on
well before the roots begin to spiral in the
containers. Coloured-leafed forms, like hybrids,
do not usually come true from seed, although
the seedlings may contain a proportion of
coloured forms
Examples: *Fagus sylvatica* (common beech);
Fagus sylvatica Atropurpurea Group (will give
a proportion of purple-leafed seedlings, so
select those with the best colour)

NAME: *FRAXINUS* (ASH)
TYPE: **DECIDUOUS TREE**

Sowing time: Autumn
Optimum temperature: Needs a cold period
before germination
Germination time: 4–5 months
Specific notes: Collect the seeds in the autumn
before they turn brown, and sow them
immediately. Seeds that have already turned
brown may take two or more years to
germinate. Seedlings emerging early in the
spring should be protected from hard frosts
Examples: *Fraxinus excelsior* (common ash);
Fraxinus ornus (manna ash)

NAME: *JUGLANS* (WALNUT)
TYPE: **DECIDUOUS TREE**

Sowing time: Autumn
Optimum temperature: A cold period is
beneficial
Germination time: 4–5 months
Specific notes: Collect the seed as it falls in
autumn and remove the nut from the outer husk.
Sow the seed in individual deep pots in a cold
frame. Protect from rodents. The young
seedlings should be protected from frosts when
they emerge in the spring. Pot on or plant out
the seedlings before the roots begin to spiral.
Unlike other large seeds, the nuts can be
stored in moist peat at a low temperature for
up to 12 months
Examples: *Juglans regia* (common walnut);
Juglans nigra (black walnut)

NAME: *LAVANDULA* (LAVENDER)
TYPE: **EVERGREEN SHRUB**

Sowing time: Mid-spring
Optimum temperature: 10–15°C (50–59°F)
Germination time: 3–6 weeks
Specific notes: Lavender germinates freely from
seed but only the species, which are generally
less desirable than hybrid forms, will come
true. Some hybrids are available as

ABOVE **Shoot of *Pinus mugo* raised from seed**

commercial seed, but the seedlings are usually very variable and need careful selection to ensure they produce evenly grown plants, particularly for hedges

Examples: *Lavandula lanata; Lavandula dentata* and *L. stoechas* (French lavender)

NAME: *PAULOWNIA*
TYPE: **DECIDUOUS TREE**

Sowing time: Early spring
Optimum temperature: 10–15°C (50–59°F)
Germination time: 4–6 weeks
Specific notes: The light fluffy seeds germinate freely. Sow thinly into a seed tray in the greenhouse. The seedlings grow very rapidly and should be potted up as soon as they are large enough to handle. Young trees can reach 2m (6ft) in their second year, and the highly decorative leaves are up to 60cm (2ft) across.

However it may take several years before seed-raised plants get to the stage whereby flowering becomes a regular occurrence
Examples: *Paulownia tomentosa* (foxglove tree)

NAME: *PICEA* (SPRUCE)
TYPE: **CONIFER**

Sowing time: Autumn
Optimum temperature: Needs a cold period
Germination time: 4–5 months
Specific notes: Collect the cones from the tree before they open and place them on a tray to dry. Shake the seeds from the cones once they have opened. Sow the seeds into pans in a cold frame immediately. Purchased seed is best mixed with moist peat and stored in a fridge for 6–8 weeks before sowing
Examples: *Picea abies* (Norway spruce); *Picea omorika* (Serbian spruce)

NAME: *PINUS (PINE)*
TYPE: **CONIFER**

Sowing time: Autumn

Optimum temperature: Most species benefit from a cold period

Germination time: 4–5 months

Specific notes: Pine cones should be collected before they open and placed in a tray to collect the seeds which will fall from the cones as they dry. The seed should then be sown immediately. We have had good results with purchased seed of dwarf species such as *Pinus mugo* sown in a cold frame in autumn

Examples: *Pinus sylvestris* (Scots pine); *Pinus mugo* (mountain pine)

NAME: *PTELEA*
TYPE: **DECIDUOUS TREE**

Sowing time: Autumn

Optimum temperature: Benefits from a cold period before sowing

Germination time: 4–5 months

Specific notes: Fresh seed sown immediately will germinate freely the following spring. Seed from the green form will occasionally produce golden-leafed seedlings

Example: *Ptelea trifoliata* (hop tree)

NAME: *QUERCUS (OAK)*
TYPE: **LARGE TREES: MAINLY DECIDUOUS, SOME EVERGREEN**

Sowing time: Autumn, straight after harvest

Optimum temperature: 5–15°C (41–59°F)

Germination time: 4–8 weeks

Specific notes: Fresh healthy seed will germinate surprisingly quickly, usually before the winter sets in. Sow the acorns into individual deep containers. Oaks produce long tap roots, and growth can be significantly stunted if these roots are damaged or restricted when young. Ideally, the seedlings should be planted out within 12–24 months of germination. It is a good

idea to protect the seed from rodents

Examples: *Quercus robur* (common or English oak); *Quercus ilex* (Holm oak)

NAME: *ROSA (ROSE)*
TYPE: **DECIDUOUS SHRUB**

Sowing time: Autumn

Optimum temperature: Most species require a cold period

Germination time: 4–5 months

Specific notes: Collect the hips as they ripen. Remove the seeds from the husks by crushing and then washing through a coarse sieve. The seeds can then be sown in a deep pan and placed in a cold frame. Some species may take 18 months to germinate

Examples: *Rosa canina* (dog rose); *Rosa multiflora*; *Rosa rugosa*

NAME: *SOPHORA*
TYPE: **DECIDUOUS SHRUB**

Sowing time: Late winter

Optimum temperature: 5–10°C (41–50°F)

Germination time: 2–4 weeks

Specific notes: Collect the pods in autumn before they split. Extract the seeds from the pods and store in cool conditions over the winter. Soaking in tepid water overnight can improve germination of some species

Examples: *Sophora japonica* (Japanese pagoda tree); *Sophora prostrata*

NAME: *SORBUS*
TYPE: **DECIDUOUS TREE**

Sowing time: Autumn

Optimum temperature: Cold period required

Germination time: 4–5 months

Specific needs: To avoid lengthy dormancy, fresh seed should be used. Collect the seeds from the tree when the fruit begins to show colour. Extract the seeds from the flesh by crushing and then washing the fleshy pulp away. Sow immediately into pans of compost in a cold frame.

ABOVE **The seed of oak, *Quercus robur*, is the acorn enclosed in its cupule**

Germination can be variable – sow plenty of seed to be sure of getting several seedlings
Examples: *Sorbus aria* (whitebeam); *Sorbus hupehensis*; *Sorbus vilmorinii*

MORE UNUSUAL OR CHALLENGING TREES AND SHRUBS

NAME: *ACER* (MAPLE)
TYPE: DECIDUOUS TREE

Sowing time: Autumn
Optimum temperature: 5–10°C (41–50°F)
Germination time: 4–5 months
Specific notes: Seeds of most species will germinate readily if collected and sown before they dry out (just as they begin to change colour from green). Fresh seed can be stored over the winter in moist peat in a fridge and then sown in spring. Seed that has dried or been purchased will need the same treatment but may take up to two years to germinate. Many species will come true from seed, but others, particularly some of the snake bark and Japanese maples, will hybridize and produce variable seedlings
Examples: *Acer palmatum*; *Acer davidii*; Acer *buergerianum* and Acer *campestre* (field maple)

NAME: *CALLISTEMON* (BOTTLEBRUSH)
TYPE: EVERGREEN SHRUB

Sowing time: Early to mid-spring
Optimum temperature: 15–20°C (59–68°F)
Germination time: 2–6 weeks
Specific notes: In order to ripen fully, the seed usually needs a full 12 months from the time of flowering. Remove the seed capsules and sow the seed on the surface of the moistened compost in a prepared seed pan. It is a good idea to cover the top of the compost with a thin layer of fine grit
Examples: *Callistemon citrinus*; *C. rigidus*

ABOVE *Acer buergerianum* is an attractive species to raise from seed

NAME: *CORNUS (DOGWOOD)*
TYPE: **DECIDUOUS TREES/SHRUBS**

Sowing time: Autumn
Optimum temperature: Needs a cold period
Germination time: 4–5 months
Specific notes: Collect the seed and extract from the fleshy fruits as soon as they change colour, then sow immediately. Purchased seed will have developed a hard seed-coat and will usually need to be left an additional 12 months before it will germinate
Examples: *Cornus alba; Cornus mas; Cornus nuttallii*

NAME: *DAPHNE*
TYPE: **MAINLY EVERGREEN SHRUBS**

Sowing time: Mid-summer to early autumn
Optimum temperature: Needs a cold period
Germination time: 4–5 months but variable
Specific notes: Collect the fruits while they are still green, and then extract and sow the seed immediately. Place seed pans in a cold frame. Germination is variable and some species may need an extra year before they germinate. The percentage germination is normally low, therefore sow plenty of seed if available
Examples: *Daphne mezereum; Daphne alpina*

NAME: *DAVIDIA*
TYPE: **DECIDUOUS TREE**

Sowing time: Autumn
Optimum temperature: Needs stratification
Germination time: 16–18 months
Specific notes: Collect the seeds in the autumn and pack them into a container of moist sand. Leave in a cold shed until the following autumn when seeds showing the first signs of germination can be separated out and sown individually into deep pots. Leave these in a cold frame over-winter. The shoots will begin to appear in spring. Harden the seedlings off carefully before planting out or potting on
Examples: *Davidia involucrata* (handkerchief tree)

NAME: *LIRIODENDRON*
TYPE: **DECIDUOUS TREE**

Sowing time: Late autumn
Optimum temperature: Needs a cold period
Germination time: Fresh seed takes 4–5 months, dry seed takes 15–18 months
Specific notes: Sow the seeds into seed pans in a cold frame. Purchased seed usually needs a season of warm and then cold conditions before germination. Once the first signs of germination are seen, moving the pans onto a warm propagating bench can improve the final germination rate
Example: *Liriodendron tulipifera* (tulip tree)

NAME: *MORUS* (MULBERRY)
TYPE: **DECIDUOUS TREE**

Sowing time: Autumn
Optimum temperature: Needs a short period of cold prior to germination
Germination time: 4–5 months
Specific notes: Crush the ripe fruits and wash through a sieve to extract the small seeds. Sow into pans in a cold frame. The seeds usually germinate freely and should be sown thinly to avoid producing spindly seedlings. The mulberry seedlings grow quickly and can often be large enough to plant out by the autumn of their first season. The seed stores for a short period and purchased seed germinates well if sown in the autumn
Examples: *Morus alba* (white mulberry); *Morus nigra* (black mulberry)

NAME: *NOTHOFAGUS* (SOUTHERN BEECH)
TYPE: **EVERGREEN AND DECIDUOUS TREES**

Sowing time: Autumn
Optimum temperature: Benefits from a cold period prior to germination
Germination time: 4–5 months
Specific notes: Collect the seed as soon as it falls or pick the nutlets from the tree just before they split. Sow the seed into individual pots in a cold frame. Seed can be stored in moist peat if necessary but viability of the seed declines rapidly if it dries out
Examples: *Nothofagus nervosa*; *N. antarctica*

NAME: *TAXUS* (YEW)
TYPE: **EVERGREEN TREE**

Sowing time: Early spring
Optimum temperature: Stratification is required
Germination time: 8–12 weeks
Specific notes: Collect the berries as they ripen in autumn and extract the seed by crushing and washing. Mix the seed with moist peat in a container and store in an unheated shed for two winters. To break dormancy the seeds need a warm period – moving them to a greenhouse during the summer can help this process. Sow the seed the following spring into deep trays in a cold frame
Example: *Taxus baccata* (common yew)

NAME: *VACCINIUM*
TYPE: **EVERGREEN SHRUB**

Sowing time: Early spring
Optimum temperature: 15–20°C (59–68°F)
Germination time: 4–6 weeks
Specific needs: Sow the seeds on the surface of the compost and cover with a very thin layer of fine grit. Keep the seed moist by misting regularly until it begins to germinate
Examples: *Vaccinium ovatum* (box blueberry); *Vaccinium parvifolium* (red huckleberry)

LEFT Glowing autumn colour of a seed-raised *Acer palmatum*

CHAPTER 8

Vegetables from seed

WHAT ARE VEGETABLES?

Vegetables are a very diverse group of plants that have originated from many different climates and have been intensively bred to produce heavier or better tasting crops. The majority of them are annuals or biennials while a few, such as the runner bean, are perennials that are grown as annuals. One or two are perennials that crop for several years once established.

USES IN THE GARDEN

While vegetables are primarily grown to eat, many are also very attractive and can be grown very effectively in the ornamental garden. Even the smallest garden can accommodate vegetables grown in this way. Why plant ornamental cabbages when you could plant the attractive edible varieties, such as 'January King', instead?

The range of vegetable varieties available increases every year, with new introductions and also the reintroduction of old varieties. Many of the newer varieties are F1 hybrids that have been bred for commercial use. In most cases this means a heavy crop, all maturing together at the same time. In the garden this can mean a glut of produce for a short period rather than the steady cropping over a period of time that many of the older varieties produce.

On the other hand, with crops such as sweetcorn or tomatoes, where the harvest season is naturally fairly short, F1 hybrids can have considerable benefits.

GROWING REQUIREMENTS

Vegetables can be established using several different methods. The best method may alter over the season according to the weather and soil conditions. Early in the season, many vegetables are best started under cover and planted out when the weather improves. The traditional methods of sowing into trays and then pricking out the seedlings is very effective, but is time-consuming and introduces an extra check to growth.

For most vegetables we now prefer to sow directly into modules or cell trays and then allow the seedlings to develop without disturbance until they are planted out. Using modules requires a little bit more space initially but speeds up the process considerably. In order to end up with one seedling in each cell, two or three seeds should be sown and then the two weakest seedlings carefully removed once they have germinated.

On heavy soils where it can be difficult to produce a fine seedbed, many crops are best started in pots or modules throughout the year, which will avoid the need to create seedbeds outside. Where space is limited, sowing into modules means that the soil outside is not occupied for so long, allowing more vegetables

ABOVE **Many vegetables can be sown under cover either directly into cell trays or into pots**

to be grown in the same space over the season. The spacing of vegetable plants can have a considerable influence on the final size of the crop. For example, onions that are grown close together will produce a large number of small bulbs, while at wider spacings larger bulbs will be produced.

Sowing several seeds into a module and planting out the whole clump can have a similar effect, and crops of mini-vegetables such as leeks and beetroot can easily be produced in this way. With leaf vegetables, such as lettuce, close spacing will produce a heavy crop of young leaves, rather than individual heads.

The suggestions in the plant list that follows are based on our own experience, but with edible crops it is always worth experimenting with your own ideas.

The recommended length of time to store vegetable seeds – in other words their viability – has been included in each example.

POPULAR VEGETABLES

NAME: **BEETROOT**
TYPE: **BIENNIAL**

Sowing time: Early spring to summer
Optimum temperature: Germination is poor below 7°C (44°F)
Germination time: 10–21 days depending on soil temperature
Specific notes: Low temperatures can cause bolting. Use bolt-resistant varieties under cloches for early sowings. Can also be sown in modules in the greenhouse and planted out when the weather warms up. Beetroot 'seeds' are usually clusters of two or more seeds so even when sown individually you will often have two or more seedlings at each station
Seed storage time: 2 years
Examples: Bolt-resistant – 'Boltardy', 'Bonel'. Others – 'Red Ace F1', 'Burpees Golden' (has golden-coloured flesh)

ABOVE **Vegetables can be sown earlier outside by providing a cloche for protection**

NAME: **BROAD BEANS**
TYPE: **ANNUAL**

Sowing time: Early to mid-spring. Hardy varieties can be sown in early winter to overwinter

Optimum temperature: Germination is slower below 10°C (50°F)

Germination time: 5–10 days inside; up to 21 days outside

Specific notes: Heavier crops and disease-free plants usually result from early sowings. In cold areas or on wet soils, sow in individual pots in a greenhouse in late winter and plant out in early spring after hardening off well

Seed storage time: 2 years

Examples: Hardy variety – 'Aquadulce'. Other excellent forms include – 'The Sutton', 'Bunyards Exhibition', 'Express'

NAME: **CABBAGE**
TYPE: **BIENNIAL**

Sowing time: Late winter to early autumn depending on variety

Optimum temperature: 10–18°C (50–66°F)

Germination time: 7–14 days

Specific notes: Cabbage should be sown in a seedbed or in containers and transplanted when large enough to handle. Seed germinates readily so sow thinly to avoid overcrowding. Cabbage seedlings dislike high temperatures so shade cold frames and greenhouses in hot weather

Seed storage time: 4 years

Examples: 'Hispi' (pointed early variety), 'Minicole' (late white cabbage), 'January King' (crinkle-leafed winter cabbage), 'Durham Early' (early semi-hearted spring cabbage)

ABOVE **Sowing directly into modules means these French bean seedlings can develop undisturbed until ready for planting**

NAME: **CARROT**
TYPE: **BIENNIAL**

Sowing time: Early spring to summer. Sow in succession for cropping through the summer and into winter
Optimum temperature: 8°C (46°F)
Germination time: 10–21 days or longer in cold soils
Specific notes: Carrots do not transplant; they should be sown in their cropping position. Early crops can be grown under cloches. They can also be grown successfully in large pots of potting compost. The round varieties, such as 'Rondo', can be sown in modules and planted out while still young
Seed storage time: 3 years
Examples: 'Amsterdam Forcing' (very early), 'Flyaway F1' (resistant to carrot fly), 'Autumn King' (maincrop variety)

NAME: **CELERY**
TYPE: **BIENNIAL**

Sowing time: Early spring in seed trays inside
Optimum temperature: 10–13°C (50–55°F)
Germination time: 14–21 days
Specific notes: The seed needs light to germinate; sow on the surface of a fine potting compost and keep moist. Seedlings should be pricked out into trays or modules before planting out in late spring. Avoid checks to growth, which can lead to bolting
Seed storage time: 3 years
Examples: 'Lathom' (self-blanching), 'Victoria F1' (quick-maturing green variety)

ABOVE **A few seeds have been sown in each cell to produce a clump of seedlings, an ideal technique for mini-vegetables or leaf salads**

NAME: **COURGETTE/MARROW**
TYPE: **ANNUAL**

Sowing time: Spring in pots indoors, early summer outdoors
Optimum temperature: 20–25°C (68–77°F)
Germination time: 7–10 days
Specific notes: Sow individual seeds on their edges in 9cm (3.5in) pots in spring and plant out after last frosts. Courgettes and marrows resent root disturbance, so plant out or pot on before they become pot-bound
Seed storage time: 5 years
Examples: Although marrows and courgettes are very similar, the best results are achieved using varieties bred for each specific use. Courgettes: 'Defender F1', 'Zucchini', 'Gold Rush F1'. Marrows: 'Green Bush', 'Tiger Cross F1'

NAME: **CUCUMBER**
TYPE: **ANNUAL**

Sowing time: Early spring for indoor crop, late spring for outside cropping
Optimum temperature: 20–25°C (68–77°F)
Germination time: 7–10 days
Specific notes: Sow seeds on their edges, two to a 9cm (3.5in) pot. Once they germinate remove the weakest of the pair. Keep the seedlings growing steadily, potting on if necessary before planting out
Seed storage time: 5 years
Examples: Greenhouse varieties: All female F1 types give the best results – 'Petita F1' (short half-length fruit), 'Femspot F1'. Outdoor ridge varieties: 'Burpless Tasty Green F1', 'Marketmore', 'Crystal Apple' (interesting round fruit)

NAME: **LEEK**
TYPE: **BIENNIAL**

Sowing time: Early spring under glass or late spring outside

Optimum temperature: 18–20°C (66–68°F)

Germination time: 7–14 days

Specific notes: Early spring sowings of leeks should be pricked out into trays or modules and they should grow to pencil thickness before planting out. Plant out by summer at the latest to reduce bolting. Can be multi-sown in modules to produce mini-leeks

Seed storage time: 3 years

Examples: In order of maturity – 'Carlton F1', 'Snowstar', 'Musselburgh', 'Newton F1'. For mini-leeks use 'Jolant'

ABOVE **Each of these beetroot 'seeds' is a cluster of two or more seeds**

NAME: **LETTUCE**
TYPE: **BIENNIAL**

Sowing time: Early spring to early autumn depending on variety

Optimum temperature: 20°C (68°F)

Germination time: 4–10 days

Specific notes: Lettuce germination can be poor at temperatures above 25°C (77°F). Mid-summer sowings are best done in the shade or in the evening, so the first stage of germination can occur in the cooler night temperatures. We found that covering seed trays with a piece of expanded polystyrene until germination begins is very effective

Seed storage time: 3 years

Examples: For loose leaves – 'Bijou', 'Lollo Bionda'; Iceberg types – 'Lakeland', 'Webbs Wonderful'; Butterhead types – 'All The Year Round', 'Clarion'; late season – 'Valdor'

NAME: **ONIONS**
TYPE: **BIENNIAL**

Sowing time: Late winter to spring. Sow over-wintering varieties in late autumn

Optimum temperature: 10–15°C (50–59°F)

Germination time: 7–14 days

Specific notes: For the largest bulbs start seed indoors in late winter. Sow the seed thinly in deep trays or in modules. Plant out in spring when the seedlings are well developed. Outdoor sowings should be made in the cropping position, thinning the seedlings to about 5cm (2in) apart in the row

Seed storage time: 1 year

Examples: 'The Kelsae', 'Ailsa Craig', 'Romeo F1'. Autumn Sown – 'Buffalo F1'

NAME: **PARSLEY**
TYPE: **BIENNIAL (GROWN AS AN ANNUAL FOR THE FRESH YOUNG LEAVES)**

Sowing time: Spring for summer use or late summer for winter use

Optimum temperature: 15–20°C (59–68°F)

Germination time: 14–21 days

Specific notes: Parsley has a reputation for being tricky, but we have found it is best to sow it in pots or modules inside. The compost should be kept moist all the time. Plant seedlings out once well established

Seed storage time: 1 year

Examples: Curled leaves – 'Bravour', 'Moss Curled'. Flat leaf – 'Giant of Italy'

ABOVE **These broad beans have been started in individual pots in a greenhouse**

NAME: **PEAS**
TYPE: **ANNUAL**

Sowing time: Early spring to mid-summer
Optimum temperature: 5–25°C (41–77°F)
Germination time: 7–21 days, depending on the temperature
Specific notes: Germination will be hastened if the seeds are soaked for a few hours before sowing. We have had considerable success with early crops sown in modules under cover, and then planted out before the roots become tightly packed. Outdoor sowings may need protection from mice
Seed storage time: 2 years
Examples: Early varieties – 'Feltham First', 'Meteor'. Maincrop – 'Bayard' (a semi-leafless type), 'Onward', 'Cavalier'

NAME: **PEPPERS**
TYPE: **ANNUAL**

Sowing time: Early to mid-spring
Optimum temperature: 20–25°C (68–77°F)
Germination time: 10–14 days
Specific notes: Peppers need warm conditions and are therefore best grown under cover. Sow seed in pots or small trays and prick out into individual pots when large enough to handle. Pot on as required
Seed storage time: 2 years
Examples: Sweet peppers – 'Gypsy F1', 'New Ace', 'Sweet Banana'. Chilli peppers – 'Hungarian Hot Wax', 'Cayenne'

ABOVE A 'January King' cabbage ready for harvesting

NAME: **RADISH**
TYPE: **ANNUAL**

Sowing time: Late winter to early autumn
Optimum temperature: 5–25°C (41–77°F)
Germination time: 3–10 days
Specific notes: Seed should be sown in situ and thinned to about 2cm (¾in) apart as soon as the seedlings are large enough to handle. Early crops can be grown in large pots in a greenhouse or cold frame. Flea beetles often cause damage to late spring and summer sowings – we have found that covering the seedbed with fleece immediately after sowing is a very effective control
Seed storage time: 4 years
Examples: 'Jolly F1', 'Cherry Belle', 'French Breakfast' (an old favourite but still excellent)

NAME: **RUNNER BEANS**
TYPE: **PERENNIAL** (GROWN AS AN ANNUAL)

Sowing time: Mid-spring inside, or late spring to early summer outside
Optimum temperature: 10–20°C (50–68°F)
Germination time: 3–14 days
Specific notes: Soaking the seeds in water overnight before sowing can speed up germination. For best results the seeds should be sown on their edges, not flat. Early sowings should be made in individual pots under cover, which should then be hardened off before planting out after the last frosts
Seed storage time: 2 years
Examples: 'Scarlet Emperor', 'Achievement', 'Polestar', 'Hestia' (dwarf variety, very good for growing in containers)

NAME: **SPINACH**
TYPE: **ANNUAL**

Sowing time: Early to late spring for summer crop. Late summer to early autumn for late crop
Optimum temperature: 8–20°C (46–68°F)
Germination time: 7–14 days
Specific notes: Sow thinly in rows to avoid the need to thin out. Sow a small area every 14 days to ensure a regular crop through the season. Keep the seedlings moist to prevent premature bolting
Seed storage time: 3 years
Examples: 'Spinnaker F1', 'Medina'

NAME: **SWEDE**
TYPE: **BIENNIAL**

Sowing time: Late spring to early summer
Optimum temperature: 12–25°C (54–77°F)
Germination time: 7–14 days
Specific notes: The use of resistant varieties and late spring sowing will help to avoid problems with powdery mildew. Seedlings should be kept well watered to prevent the roots becoming woody. Thin the seedlings as soon as they are large enough to handle
Seed storage time: 4 years
Examples: Mildew-resistant types – 'Marian', 'Invitation'. Others – 'Brora', 'Melfort'

NAME: **SWEETCORN**
TYPE: **ANNUAL**

Sowing time: Mid to late spring inside or early summer outside
Optimum temperature: Minimum 15°C (59°F)
Germination time: 10–14 days
Specific notes: Root damage is detrimental to the plants, so indoor sowings should be made in pots. These should be planted out in early summer, taking care not to damage the roots

LEFT Mild-flavoured mini-leeks 'Jolant', which can be multi-sown and planted out as small clumps

Outdoor sowing can be made as soon as the soil is warm enough. Sowing or planting out in a block will improve pollination and produce full cobs
Seed storage time: 1 year
Examples: 'Champ F1', 'Incredible F1'. For mini cobs – 'Mini Pop F1'

NAME: **TOMATO**
TYPE: **ANNUAL**

Sowing time: Early spring
Optimum temperature: 20–25°C (68–77°F)
Germination time: 10–21 days
Specific notes: Once the seed has germinated the temperature should be reduced, particularly during dull weather, as high temperatures and low light levels will produce spindly seedlings. Seedlings should be pricked out into individual pots as soon as the first true leaves appear. Keep the plants growing steadily as early checks in growth can have a significant adverse effect on cropping
Seed storage time: 3 years
Examples: 'Shirley F1', 'Ailsa Craig', 'Vanessa F1', 'Moneymaker'. Small cherry tomatoes – 'Gardener's Delight', 'Sungold F1'. Beefsteak varieties – 'Super Marmande', 'Big Boy'

NAME: **TURNIP**
TYPE: **ANNUAL**

Sowing time: Early spring to late summer
Optimum temperature: 10–25°C (50–77°F)
Germination time: 7–14 days
Specific notes: Regular sowings through the year will produce a continuous crop of fresh young roots. Keep the seedlings and plants moist to prevent the roots turning woody. Flea beetle attack from late spring to late summer can be prevented by covering the seedbed with horticultural fleece
Seed storage time: 4 years
Examples: 'Purple Top Milan', 'Snowball', 'Tokyo Cross F1'

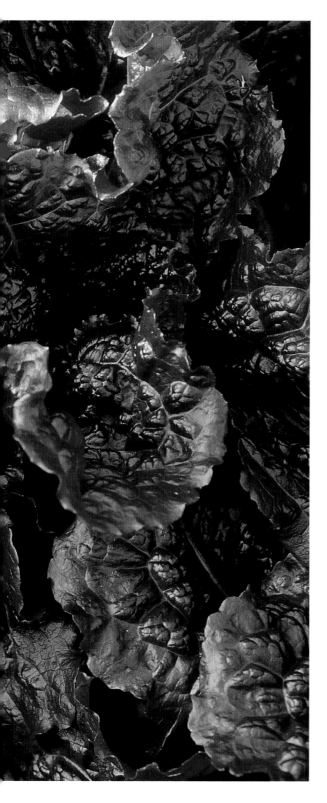

MORE UNUSUAL VEGETABLES

NAME: **ARTICHOKE (GLOBE)**
TYPE: **PERENNIAL**

Sowing time: Early to mid-spring
Optimum temperature: 18–25°C (66–77°F)
Germination time: 7–14 days
Specific notes: Sow in trays under glass and prick out the seedlings into 9cm (3.5in) pots. Plant outside in early summer, spacing the plants 1x1m (3x3ft). They should be fed and watered well through their first season. Cropping should commence in late summer or early autumn of the second season. The plants are very decorative and can look effective grown in the flower border
Seed storage time: 2 years
Example: 'Green Globe'

NAME: **ASPARAGUS PEAS**
TYPE: **ANNUAL**

Sowing time: Mid to late spring
Optimum temperature: 15–20°C (59–68°F)
Germination time: 7–14 days
Specific notes: Needs a warm fertile soil that does not dry out. Sow in rows and thin out to about 15cm (6in) apart. We have found that these peas do not like being transplanted. Pods should be picked when they are very young for the best flavour
Seed storage time: 2 years
Examples: No named varieties

LEFT **Grow contrasting lettuces together – these are green 'All The Year Round' and dark red 'Bijou'**

NAME: **AUBERGINE**
TYPE: **ANNUAL**

Sowing time: Late winter to early spring
Optimum temperature: 18–25°C (66–77°F)
Germination time: 14–21 days
Specific notes: Aubergines need warm conditions to crop well and are best grown under glass or plastic. Early sown seeds will produce heavier crops, but the plants will need to be kept in warm conditions until late spring. Sow in seed trays and prick out into 9cm (3.5in) pots, finally planting into growing bags or 25cm (10in) pots in early summer
Seed storage time: 3 years
Examples: 'Moneymaker F1', 'Black Beauty'

NAME: **CELERIAC**
TYPE: **BIENNIAL**

Sowing time: Early spring
Optimum temperature: 20–25°C (68–77°F)
Germination time: 14–21 days
Specific notes: Celeriac needs a long growing season to produce good-sized roots. Sow under glass in trays and cover only with a fine layer of vermiculite to allow some light through. Prick out into large modules when large enough to handle, and maintain warm conditions. The seedlings should be kept moist but not wet. Plant out in late spring after hardening off, spacing the plants 30x30cm (12x12in)
Seed storage time: 3 years
Examples: 'Alabaster', 'Monarch'

LEFT A crisp curled-leaf lettuce, 'Frillice', for harvesting as whole heads or a few leaves at a time

NAME: **CHICORY – WITLOOF**
TYPE: **BIENNIAL**

Sowing time: Late spring to early summer
Optimum temperature: 15–20°C (59–68°F)
Germination time: 7–14 days
Specific notes: Chicory must not be sown too early as low temperatures will induce bolting. Sow directly into the ground, thinning the seedlings to about 15cm (6in) apart. Once the night temperatures approach freezing the roots can be lifted for forcing indoors. The roots are packed into pots of potting compost, with a space of 15–20cm (6–8in) above, and then placed in complete darkness for the blanched chicons to develop
Seed storage time: 4 years
Example: 'Witloof'

NAME: **CHIVES**
TYPE: **PERENNIAL**

Sowing time: Early spring
Optimum temperature: 10°C (50°F)
Germination time: 7–21 days
Specific notes: Chives germinate easily, either in rows outside or under glass. We prefer to sow under cover in modules. By sowing several seeds in each cell good clumps are produced which can then be planted out directly into their final growing positions
Seed storage time: 1 year
Examples: No named varieties

NAME: **FLORENCE FENNEL**
TYPE: **ANNUAL**

Sowing time: Mid-spring to mid-summer
Optimum temperature: 10–25°C (50–77°F)
Germination time: 10–21 days. Can be very erratic, particularly at low temperatures
Specific notes: Sow in rows, thinning out to 20cm (8in) apart. Regular watering is

LEFT **Maincrop onion 'Sturon'**

ABOVE **Runner bean pods**

essential, particularly in hot weather, or the plants will bolt. It is possible to sow into modules under glass for an earlier crop but the seedlings must be planted out while young or they will all bolt
Seed storage time: 2 years
Examples: 'Zefa Fino', 'Amigo F1'

123

ABOVE **Chives make an attractive edging, as well as yielding edible leaves**

NAME: **KOHL RABI**
TYPE: **BIENNIAL**

Sowing time: Mid-spring to mid-summer
Optimum temperature: 10–25°C (50–77°F)
Germination time: 7–14 days
Specific notes: Sow regularly over the season for a succession of tender young roots. For larger roots, sow under cover in early spring in modules and pot into 9cm (3.5in) pots when the seedlings are large enough to handle. After hardening off the young plants, set them outside in rich fertile soil during late spring
Seed storage time: 4 years
Examples: 'Kolibri F1', 'Blusta'

NAME: **MELON**
TYPE: **ANNUAL**

Sowing time: From late winter to late spring under cover
Optimum temperature: 20–25°C (68–77°F)
Germination time: 7–14 days
Specific notes: Sow seeds on their edges into

LEFT **A truss of ripening tomatoes**

9cm (3.5in) pots of seed compost. They should be potted on before the pots become full of roots. Plant out into frames or growing bags in early summer. In colder areas choose early maturing varieties to ensure good crops
Seed storage time: 5 years
Examples: 'Sweetheart F1', 'Passport F1', 'Major F1' (all early maturing)

NAME: **PAK CHOI**
TYPE: **BIENNIAL**

Sowing time: Early to late summer
Optimum temperature: 18–20°C (66–68°F)
Germination time: 3–7days
Specific notes: Low temperatures can cause bolting. For early crops sow in modules under glass and plant out when the temperature is at least 15°C (59°F). This must, however, be done before the modules become full of roots. To ensure a continuous crop sow short rows every 14 days through the summer. Thin the seedlings to 10–15cm (4–6in) apart
Seed storage time: 2 years
Examples: 'Mei Qing Choi F1' (very good bolting resistance), 'Joi Choi F1'

CHAPTER 9

Climbers, bulbs and houseplants from seed

INTRODUCTION

There are many types of plants, other than those discussed in the preceding chapters, that can be raised from seed. Examples include annual and woody climbing plants, hardy and half-hardy bulbs, houseplants, cacti, aquatic plants and grasses. In this chapter we shall concentrate on the first three categories only.

To obtain seed of these less common plants, you may need to search for specialist suppliers, though the popular commercial suppliers are becoming more diverse in the ranges they stock. Scan the advertisements at the back of gardening magazines or in the journals of specialist plant societies, where you are likely to find contacts for seed companies both in the UK and abroad.

CLIMBERS

Climbing plants provide a vertical element to gardens, covering supports of various kinds. Annual, herbaceous or woody climbers all add distinctive structure, foliage and colour, whether trained up walls, fences, trellis, pergolas or tripods, or allowed to scramble through shrubs and trees. Grow late-flowering climbers through earlier-flowering shrubs to extend the flowering season, or train two or more climbers through each other.

Growing perennial or shrubby climbers from seed requires patience, as it takes some time for the plants to grow sufficiently and reach flowering size. On the other hand, annual climbers put on incredible amounts of growth in one year, providing an effective, though relatively short-term display. They are well worth raising from seed, as they allow you to introduce height and colour in different places each year, or to create cover while waiting for more permanent plants to establish.

GROWING REQUIREMENTS

Raising from seed is the only practical way of propagating annual climbers, but it is also a cost-effective method of increasing your stock of other climbing plants. Remember that hybrids and cultivars seldom come true from seed, so these are best propagated vegetatively.

Seeds with hard outer coats are best soaked in water overnight, and seeds of many hardy climbers require a cold period for up to eight weeks after sowing. Space out large seeds evenly and cover with a layer of compost and then a layer of grit. Press small seeds gently into compost and cover simply with a layer of fine grit.

Seed of hardy climbers, including annual sweet peas, can be kept outside or in a cold frame, bringing into warmer conditions once germination occurs. Most annual, tender climbers require heat for successful germination.

Prick out seedlings once the first pair of true leaves emerges; these often differ markedly from the seedling's first leaves. If the seedlings are large

ABOVE **Distinctive fluffy seed-head of** *Clematis tangutica*

enough, use individual pots, otherwise use modules or trays. Pot on as necessary and keep young plants growing steadily until established. Provide a cane in each pot and tie shoots up to prevent them getting tangled. Plant out tender half-hardy climbers once all danger of frost is over. Grow woody climbers on for a season or two, potting on as necessary, before planting out.

CLIMBERS TO RAISE FROM SEED

NAME: *ASARINA* (TWINING SNAPDRAGON)
TYPE: **HALF-HARDY ANNUAL** (HHP TREAT AS HHA)

Sowing time: Late winter to mid-spring inside
Optimum temperature: 18–20°C (66–68°F)
Germination time: 21–30 days
Specific notes: Germinate rapidly. Lovely climbers for a sunny patio, conservatory or cool greenhouse
Examples: *Asarina wislizensis* 'Red Dragon', large tubular carmine flowers, 1.2m (4ft); *A. scandens* 'Jewel Mixed', violet blue, pink or white, 1.2–2m (4–6ft). Flowering mid-summer to mid-autumn

NAME: *CLEMATIS*
TYPE: **HARDY PERENNIAL/SHRUB**

Sowing time: Mid-winter to early spring, or autumn for freshly collected seeds
Optimum temperature: Cold frame
Germination time: 30 days to 9 months
Specific notes: Seed requires a cold period (except *C. tangutica*). Sow thinly in gritty compost and cover with grit, placing in a cold frame or outside. Bring into warmer conditions once germination begins. Pot up seedlings individually once large enough to handle, when they have developed the first pair of true leaves. Grow on for a season or two until well established
Examples: *Clematis alpina*, dainty blue flowers in spring, up to 3m (10ft); *C. tangutica* x *hybridus* 'Helios', bright yellow flowers mid-summer to mid-autumn, can flower first year from early sowing, 3m (10ft); *C. macropetala*, semi-double violet blue, early summer, 3m (10ft)

NAME: *COBAEA (CATHEDRAL BELLS)*
TYPE: **HALF-HARDY ANNUAL** (HHP TREAT AS HHA)

Sowing time: Early to mid-spring
Optimum temperature: 18–21°C (66–70°F)
Germination time: 14–21 days
Specific notes: Sow directly into individual pots early (so they are well developed when ready to plant out), then pot on and plant out when large enough and weather is warm. A lovely, vigorous, annual climber
Examples: *Cobaea scandens*, purple-flushed foliage and tendrils, purple flowers, 3–6m (10–20ft); *C. scandens alba*, a beautiful white- flowered form. Flowering takes place from mid-summer to mid-autumn

NAME: *CODONOPSIS*
TYPE: **HARDY PERENNIAL**

Sowing time: Mid-winter to early spring inside; mid-spring to early summer outside
Optimum temperature: 18–21°C (66–70°F)
Germination time: 7–40 days
Specific notes: Seeds germinate readily, and plants from an early sowing usually flower in their first year. Take care when handling, as trailing stems are slender and fragile. Pot up when seedlings are large enough to handle, and start tying to a small cane as soon as possible to prevent stems flopping and breaking. Plants will need help to start climbing when first planted out
Examples: *Codonopsis clematidea*, soft powder-blue, 50–90cm (20–36in); *C. viridiflora*, yellow-green purple-veined flowers, 2m (6ft). Flowering summer

LEFT The beautiful large flowers of *Cobaea scandens* deepen to rich purple as they mature

NAME: *ECCREMOCARPUS* (CHILEAN GLORY VINE)
TYPE: **HALF-HARDY PERENNIAL** (TREAT AS HHA)

Sowing time: Mid-winter to early spring inside
Optimum temperature: 13°C (55°F)
Germination time: 21–28 days
Specific notes: Easily grown from seed, this self-clinging climber produces numerous clusters of tubular flowers over a long period. It is often hardy in sheltered spots, and will self-seed
Examples: *Eccremocarpus scaber* 'Carnival Time', shades of yellow, orange and red, 3m (10ft); *E. scaber* 'Tresco', orange-crimson or pink-tinged cream. Flowering mid-summer to mid-autumn, longer in mild spells

ABOVE Colourful blooms of *Ipomoea lobata*

LEFT Tubular flowers of *Eccremocarpus scaber*

NAME: *IPOMOEA* (MORNING GLORY)
TYPE: **HALF-HARDY ANNUAL**

Sowing time: Early to mid-spring inside
Optimum temperature: 20–21°C (68–70°F)
Germination time: 7–21 days
Specific notes: Soak or chip seeds prior to sowing and sow directly into individual pots or deep modules to prevent root disturbance, which is detrimental to the plant. Vigorous annual climbers for large containers with support, for pergolas, arches, tripods or fences, or for scrambling over and through shrubs. Each flower only lasts half a day, but flowering is prolific on well-grown plants
Examples: *Ipomoea tricolor* 'Crimson Rambler', bright rose white-throated flowers, 3m (10ft); *I. tricolor* 'Heavenly Blue', very large clear sky-blue flowers, 3m (10ft). Also now included in this genus is *Ipomoea lobata* (syn. *Mina lobata*), masses of exotic-looking tubular flowers opening red, maturing through orange, yellow and white, 2–3m (6–10ft)

NAME: *LATHYRUS* (EVERLASTING PEA)
TYPE: HARDY PERENNIAL

Sowing time: Spring inside, late spring outside
Optimum temperature: 15–18°C (59–66°F)
Germination time: 10–21 days
Specific notes: Sow inside to produce
flowering plants earlier
Examples: *Lathyrus latifolius* 'Pink Pearl'
2.4–3m (8–10ft); *L. latifolius albus* 'White
Pearl' 1.8m (5½ft); *L. laxiflorus* (small,
scrambling sweet pea). Flowering from early
summer to autumn

NAME: *LATHYRUS* (SWEET PEA)
TYPE: HARDY ANNUAL

Sowing time: Autumn or late winter inside or
spring outside
Optimum temperature: 15–18°C (59–66°F)
Germination time: 7–21 days
Specific notes: For best results and earlier
flowering, sow in autumn in a cold frame or
unheated greenhouse to produce plants ready
for placing outside in early spring. Seed sown
in heat during late winter will be ready for
planting out in late spring. Seed can also be
sown in situ outside in spring, though plants
will begin flowering later
Examples: *Lathyrus odoratus* has numerous
cultivated hybrids, including the large-flowered
Spencer sweet peas. They are available in a
huge range of colours, often with beautifully
scented blooms that are excellent for cutting.
You will find an enormous choice in most
flower seed catalogues. As well as the usual
hybrid forms there are other annual sweet pea
species worth growing. These are ideal for
training up trellis or tripods, or for scrambling
through shrubs: *Lathyrus sativus* (azure-blue
flowers); *L. chloranthus* (lime-yellow), and
L. clymenum (tiny maroon and white blooms)

LEFT *Ipomoea tricolor* 'Crimson Rambler'

ABOVE Immature *Lathyrus* seed pod, which dries as
it ripens and twists open to release the seeds

NAME: *RHODOCHITON* (PURPLE BELL VINE)
TYPE: HALF-HARDY PERENNIAL (TREAT AS HHA)

Sowing time: Mid-winter to early spring inside
Optimum temperature: 18°C (66°F)
Germination time: 12–40 days
Specific notes: Sow early to produce flowers
for same year
Examples: *Rhodochiton atrosanguineum*, large
fan-shaped leaves, deepest purple flowers with
dusky-pink calyces, 2.4m (8ft). Flowering early
summer to autumn

NAME: *TROPAEOLUM*
TYPE: HARDY ANNUAL OR HALF-HARDY
PERENNIAL

Sowing time: Mid-winter to mid-spring inside
Optimum temperature: 10–20°C (50–68°F)
Germination time: 20 days to 12 months
Specific notes: Some species may need a cold period for up to eight weeks. Sow the annual canary creeper directly into modules or individual pots

Examples: *Tropaeolum peregrinum* (canary creeper), bright yellow fringed flowers, really fast-growing annual climber, 2–2.4m (6–8ft); *T. tricolor*, twining plant for conservatory or greenhouse, evergreen foliage and orange-red and yellow flowers, 1.5m (5ft); *T. speciosum*, vermilion flowers, needs winter protection, 3m (10ft). Flowering early summer to mid-autumn

134

BULBS

A bulb is a swollen food-storage organ enabling the plant to survive when dormant. It consists of fleshy leaves or leaf bases, and in some plants, such as *Narcissus*, the outer scales are dry and form a protective skin. A bulb puts on a display for one season, then dies away and remains dormant for the rest of the year. Propagating bulbs by seed can be interesting and fun, even though it may be a long process. The average time between sowing

and flowering is three to five years, sometimes more, occasionally less. However, if you sow some bulb seeds each year to raise different species, then once you get started, you will have a succession of stages from newly sown seed through developing bulbs, to bulbs of flowering size.

Bulbs traditionally brighten up the garden in spring, but many others flower during summer and autumn. Hardy bulbs can be planted and left to come up each year, while half-hardy and tender bulbs are best grown in pots and kept under protection in cold weather. Pots can be placed outside, either standing on hard surfaces or plunged into the ground.

Plant bulbs in groups of the same species or cultivar for maximum effect. They are excellent for seasonal displays and colour in the garden, in containers or in pots in the greenhouse. They range from tiny delicate flowers on small plants to tall majestic types for the border.

GROWING REQUIREMENTS

If you collect your own seed, either sow straight away or store the seed until autumn or spring, bearing in mind that bulb seeds tend to germinate at the time the plant naturally comes up (for instance, *Narcissus* in winter, *Habranthus* in summer). A general rule of thumb is:

● For autumn/winter/spring-flowering bulbs, sow in autumn – the seeds undergo a cold period, which is often beneficial to germination – some species will germinate in autumn, others in spring.
● For summer-flowering bulbs, sow in spring and they will germinate in summer.

Use a loam-based seed compost, such as John Innes, and sow seeds thinly as it is advisable to leave new bulbs to develop in the same pot for a whole season or two. Cover with a thin layer of compost and then flint grit. Place hardy bulb seeds outside or in a cold frame to benefit from cold weather. Once germination begins, move outside pots under cover. Feed the seedlings with a weak solution of fertilizer, and keep moist until foliage shows signs of dying down in summer (or in late autumn for summer-flowering bulbs). When it dies down, allow pots to dry out a little, but not completely (as with mature bulbs) because the tiny bulbs can shrivel too much. Start watering well again when signs of new growth are visible.

Leave seedlings for up to three years (generally two, or even one in the case of vigorous growers), feeding with half-strength liquid fertilizer during their growing season only. When large enough, pot them on during a dormant period. Tip out the whole pot and separate the bulbs, then repot individually in fresh compost and grow on for two to three seasons until large enough to plant out.

You can germinate the seed of some bulbs (large seeds such as *Lilium* and *Fritillaria*) in a plastic bag, mixed with damp vermiculite, perlite or peat. Seal the bag, label and place in a warm area such as the airing cupboard. Check frequently for signs of germination, and once a number of seeds have begun to germinate, prick out into pots or trays of compost and keep in cooler conditions (a cold greenhouse, for example).

BULBS TO RAISE FROM SEED

NAME: *ALLIUM*
TYPE: **HARDY BULB**

Sowing time: Mid-winter to early spring inside
Optimum temperature: 10–15°C (50–59°F)
Germination time: 30 days–12 months
Specific notes: Seed needs a cold period for 3–6 weeks, before bringing into warmth.
Pot up individually and allow bulbs to develop before planting out
Examples: *Allium cernuum*, lovely pink flowers in drooping heads, 30cm (12in); *Allium christophii*, strap-like leaves and star-shaped lilac flowers with a metallic sheen in very large heads, 30–40cm (12–16in). Flowering late spring to mid-summer

RIGHT *Allium cernuum* will self-seed once established

NAME: *CARDIOCRINUM*
TYPE: **HARDY BULB**

Sowing time: Mid-winter to spring
Optimum temperature: 10–15°C (50–59°F)
Germination time: Three months to two years.
Dies after flowering, so collect seed and sow
regularly every year to ensure a good
succession of plants
Specific notes: Seeds should be given a cold
period of 4–6 weeks after sowing
Example: *Cardiocrinum giganteum*, fragrant,
trumpet-shaped flowers, about 20 per stem –
spectacular plant in full bloom, 3m (10ft).
Flowering mid to late summer

NAME: *EUCOMIS* (PINEAPPLE LILY)
TYPE: **HALF-HARDY BULB**

Sowing time: Late winter to mid-spring
Optimum temperature: 15–20°C (59–68°F)
Germination time: 21–30 days
Specific notes: Readily raised from seed, but
may take some years to reach flowering size
Example: *Eucomis* 'Hybrids Mixed', lush, strap-
like foliage and strong stems bearing
pineapple-like heads of small starry flowers,
45–60cm (18–24in)

NAME: *FREESIA*
TYPE: **GREENHOUSE BULB**

Sowing time: Spring to summer
Optimum temperature: 20–25°C (68–77°F)
Germination time: 25–30 days
Specific notes: Scarify seeds between sheets
of fine sandpaper, then soak in water for 24
hours prior to sowing
Example: *Freesia* 'Super Giant Mixed', highly
scented flowers of white, yellow, purple, pink,
orange-red, 30cm (12in). Flowering spring

LEFT **Ripening seed pods of** *Eucomis*

ABOVE **Distinctive flowers of** *Fritillaria meleagris*,
the snakeshead fritillary

NAME: *FRITILLARIA* (FRITILLARY)
TYPE: **HARDY BULB**

Sowing time: Autumn, as soon as ripe
Optimum temperature: Cold frame
Germination time: 10–14 weeks
Specific notes: Soak stored or purchased
seeds in water for 24 hours. Surface sow, then
cover with grit or vermiculite. Seeds may
germinate irregularly over a long period
Examples: *Fritillaria meleagris* (snakeshead
fritillary), chequered light and dark purple,
30cm (12in); *F. michailovskyi*, brownish purple
with maroon edge, 20cm (8in)

NAME: *GALANTHUS* (SNOWDROP)
TYPE: **HARDY BULB**

Sowing time: As soon as ripe in late spring; purchased seeds in winter

Optimum temperature: Needs stratification

Germination time: 12 months or more

Specific notes: Seeds need stratifying in layers of moist sand, in a container kept outside and protected by fine mesh from birds and rodents. It may take one year or more for germination to start. Check frequently after this time for signs of germination, and once started, sow seeds immediately in normal seed compost

Examples: *Galanthus elwesii*, white, 15cm (6in); *G. nivalis*, single-flowered common snowdrop, 15cm (6in); *G. plicatus*, 20cm (8in). Flowering late winter to mid-spring, depending on variety

NAME: *HABRANTHUS*
TYPE: **MOSTLY TENDER BULBS**
(THERE ARE A FEW HARDY SPECIES)

Sowing time: Autumn when ripe; mid-winter to early spring for stored seeds

Optimum temperature: 10–20°C (50–68°F)

Germination time: 14 days to several months, depending when sown

Specific notes: Germinate in summer, when plants naturally grow. Seed is freely produced and plants flower soon from seed

Example: *Habranthus tubispathus*, solitary funnel-shaped flowers of yellow and copper, surprisingly hardy, 10–20cm (4–8in). Flowering summer to autumn

NAME: *LILIUM* (LILY)
TYPE: **HARDY OR HALF-HARDY BULB**

Sowing time: Late summer and early autumn as soon as ripe

Optimum temperature: Cold frame for epigeal lilies; alternate warm at 17–21°C (65–70°F) and cold 3–5°C (37–41°F) for hypogeal lilies

Germination time: 14 days to several months, depending on species

Specific notes: Seeds germinate irregularly over a long period. Sow in cold frame or cold greenhouse. Lilies may have hypogeal germination (root formation occurs, then a cold period is needed to stimulate leaf formation); those with epigeal germination usually emerge fairly rapidly, root and shoot formation occurring more or less simultaneously. Use peaty compost

Examples: *Lilium formosanum*, fragrant white trumpets flushed reddish, 1.2m (4ft) high; *L. martagon*, distinctive reflexed petals, soft pink flecked maroon, 1.2–1.8m (4–5½ft) high. Flowering late summer to mid-autumn

LEFT Snowdrops (*Galanthus*) take a long time to germinate

RIGHT This striking dwarf lily, *Lilium formosanum* var. *pricei*, is easily raised from seed, each seed pod containing many seeds

ABOVE *Narcissus bulbocodium* is readily seed-raised

NAME: *NARCISSUS*
TYPE: **HARDY BULB**

Sowing time: Autumn
Optimum temperature: Cold frame
Germination time: 10–14 weeks
Specific notes: Needs cold period – sow in pots, cover with grit and keep in cold frame until germination occurs
Examples: *Narcissus poeticus*, strongly fragrant white flowers with a pale yellow cup with a burgundy rim, 30–50cm (12–20in); *N. bulbocodium* (hoop petticoat narcissus), 15cm (6in). Flowering spring

NAME: *TULBAGHIA*
TYPE: **HARDY OR HALF-HARDY BULB**

Sowing time: As soon as the seed is ripe in summer; purchased or stored seed should be sown in late spring
Optimum temperature: 15–20°C (59–68°F)
Germination time: 10–30 days
Specific notes: Seeds germinate in summer, when these bulbs naturally grow. Keep mature bulbs dry in winter when resting
Examples: *Tulbaghia violacea*, mauve, 20cm (8in); *T. simmleri*, cream, 30cm (12in). Flowering summer

HOUSEPLANTS

There are many plants that can be grown in the home and conservatory, placed either singly or in groups. Temperature and light are the most important factors to consider. Move plants from windowsills at night so that they are not left between windowpane and curtain where the temperature will be colder than that in the room. Most houseplants require a bright well-lit position out of direct sun, which will quickly wilt them or cause leaves and blooms to scorch and drop.

Some houseplants have a short life, and are best grown from seed then discarded after flowering. Others can be kept for flowering again the following year, while some will produce more than one flush during a year.

GROWING REQUIREMENTS

Seeds of indoor plants are often available as hybrid F1 seed, though sowing your own collected seed can produce interesting variations. Seeds are generally sown early in the year (late winter to spring), although annual types can be sown in succession until early summer to produce several plants over a period so that you have fresh plants to replace those that have finished.

Seeds with hard coats may benefit from soaking prior to sowing, while others require chipping or abrading between sheets of fine sandpaper.

Sow the seeds in standard seed compost in trays or pots (large seeds in individual pots), covering with compost unless instructed otherwise. Very tiny seeds are best left uncovered. Cover the tray or pot with a clear propagator lid or plastic to maintain humidity. Most houseplants require warmth for germination, and a heated propagator is useful to maintain a constant temperature.

Prick out or pot up seedlings once they are large enough to handle, using a good quality potting compost. Feed with liquid houseplant fertilizer during the active growing season.

HOUSEPLANTS TO RAISE FROM SEED

NAME: *CALCEOLARIA* (SLIPPER FLOWER)
TYPE: HARDY OR HALF-HARDY PERENNIAL
(BEST TREATED AS HALF-HARDY ANNUAL)

Sowing time: Mid to late winter inside or summer in cool conditions
Optimum temperature: 15–20°C (59–68°F)
Germination time: 14–21 days
Specific notes: Sow seeds on the surface of the compost. Sow early for flowering the same year or in summer in a cool greenhouse for flowering plants the following year. Keep plants in cool conditions indoors, standing on a tray of wet pebbles to keep humidity levels high
Examples: *Calceolaria* x *hybrida* 'Sunset Mixed', shades of red, copper and yellow – free-flowering over long period, 15–20cm (6–8in); *C.* x *hybrida* 'Anytime Series', F1 hybrid, flowers in just over four months from sowing anytime, 20cm (8in)

NAME: *CELOSIA* (COCKSCOMB)
TYPE: HALF-HARDY ANNUAL

Sowing time: Spring
Optimum temperature: 20°C (68°F)
Germination time: 14–21 days
Specific notes: Easily raised from seed. Plants need cool airy conditions indoors, in full light but kept out of hot sun
Examples: *Celosia plumosa* 'Kimono Mixed', bright feathery plumed flowers in red, pink and salmon, ideal for pots, 10cm (4in); *C. argentea* var. *cristata* 'Jewel Box Mixed', crested blooms of red, pink, yellow and gold, 23cm (9in). Flowering summer

NAME: *CINERARIA*
TYPE: **HOUSEPLANT**

Sowing time: Mid-spring to late summer inside
Optimum temperature: 18–22°C (66–72°F)
Germination time: 14–21 days
Specific notes: Sow in cool greenhouse. Plants need rather exacting conditions – bright light, compost kept moist with tepid water but not too wet, and humid conditions – and are best discarded after flowering
Examples: May be found under the newer name of *Pericallis*. Try: 'Spring Glory', shades of pink and mauve, often with white centres, 25cm (10in); 'Jester Scarlet', striking scarlet with white centre, 20–25cm (8–10in)

NAME: *EXACUM* (PERSIAN OR GERMAN VIOLET)
TYPE: **HOUSEPLANT**

Sowing time: Late winter to early spring
Optimum temperature: 15–20°C (59–68°F)
Germination time: 14–21 days
Specific notes: Enchanting little plants easily raised from seed. Pot up several and keep in a cool greenhouse, bringing into the house as buds begin to open. This way, you will have a succession of flowering plants. Discard plants after flowering
Example: *Exacum affine*, masses of lilac or white flowers from mid-summer to late autumn, 15–20cm (6–8in)

NAME: *HYPOESTES* (FRECKLE FACE, POLKA DOT PLANT)
TYPE: **HOUSEPLANT** (BEST TREATED AS ANNUAL)

Sowing time: Spring
Optimum temperature: 20°C (68°F)
Germination time: 14 days
Specific notes: Easily raised from seed, these colourful foliage plants need to be pinched out regularly to maintain bushiness
Example: *Hypoestes* 'Splash Series', leaves heavily splashed with pink, red, rose or creamy white, to 30cm (12in)

NAME: *SAINTPAULIA* (AFRICAN VIOLET)
TYPE: **HOUSEPLANT OR HALF-HARDY PERENNIAL**

Sowing time: Late winter to late spring inside
Optimum temperature: 20°C (68°F)
Germination time: 21–30 days
Specific notes: Surface sow and do not cover seeds. Maintain high humidity in propagator, or cover seed tray in a layer of thin polythene. Keep seedlings and young plants out of sun and do not overwater
Examples: There are various mixtures available, with a range of flower colours, 10–20cm (4–8in). Flowering most of the year

NAME: *SINNINGIA* (GLOXINIA)
TYPE: **HALF-HARDY PERENNIAL**

Sowing time: Mid-winter to early spring inside
Optimum temperature: 18–22°C (66–72°F)
Germination time: 14–21 days
Specific notes: Sow on surface of compost and do not cover. Keep in humid conditions. Prick out into individual pots five weeks after sowing, growing on at 15–20°C (59–68°F). Keep compost moist but not too wet, and feed only with weak fertilizer. Protect leaves and flowers from strong sunlight
Example: *Sinningia* 'Empress Mixed' F1 hybrid is early flowering and comes in a range of colours, 25cm (10in)

RIGHT *Tulbaghia simmleri* has clusters of scented white flowers on tall stems

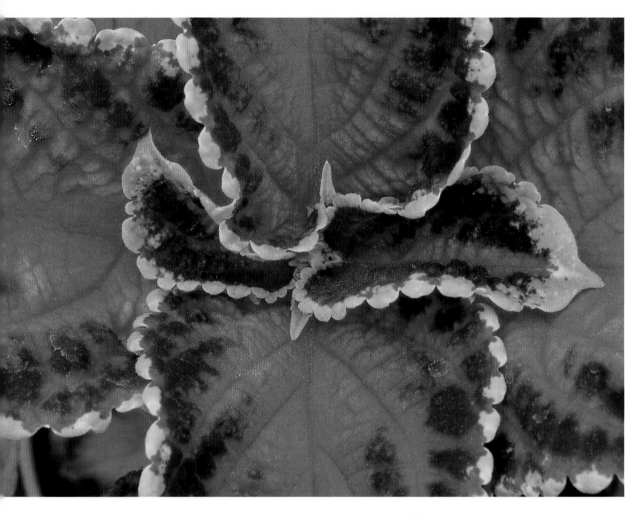

ABOVE Colourful foliage of a coleus (*Solenostemon*)

NAME: *SOLENOSTEMON* (COLEUS)
TYPE: HOUSEPLANT OR HALF-HARDY PERENNIAL

Sowing time: Late winter to mid-spring inside
Optimum temperature: 20–22°C (68–72°F)
Germination time: 10–20 days
Specific notes: Surface sow and cover lightly with vermiculite. To keep foliage at its best, remove flower spikes as they appear, and pinch out tips regularly to keep plant bushy. Widely grown as indoor plants, though also popular as container and bedding plants. Keep in bright light for best leaf colours
Examples: *Solenostemon* 'Palisandra', large, velvety, deepest purple-black leaves, 45cm (18in); 'Wizard Scarlet', compact, rich velvet red leaves edged gold, 20cm (8in); 'Flame Dancers', wide range of foliage colours and patterns, 30cm (12in)

NAME: *STREPTOCARPUS* (CAPE PRIMROSE)
TYPE: HOUSEPLANT OR HALF-HARDY PERENNIAL

Sowing time: Mid-winter to mid-spring
Optimum temperature: 20–25°C (68–77°F)
Germination time: 21–60 days
Specific notes: The seeds are tiny, so sow on

ABOVE Trumpet-shaped flower of a purple *Streptocarpus*

surface of compost and keep moist. Pot on
individually when large enough to handle.
Fairly slow growing so do not over-pot.
Can flower in first year (mid to late summer)
from a mid-winter sowing
Examples: *Streptocarpus* x *hybridus* 'Royal
Mixed', F1 hybrid, exotic trumpet-shaped
flowers in shades of pink and mauve, plus
white, with darker throat markings, 25cm
(10in); *S.* 'Windowsill Magic Mixed', F1
hybrid, purple, mauve and lilac – flowers just
four months after sowing, 30cm (12in)

NAME: *THUNBERGIA* (BLACK-EYED SUSAN)
TYPE: HALF-HARDY ANNUAL

Sowing time: Late winter to mid-spring inside
Optimum temperature: 18°C (66°F)
Germination time: 14–30 days
Specific notes: Easily raised twining plant that
makes an unusual pot plant for the home. Pinch
out tips of young plants to encourage bushiness,
and provide support for stems in a decent-sized
pot. Flowers in 12 weeks from sowing
Examples: *Thunbergia alata* 'Beauty Spots', orange,
vanilla or white flowers with chocolate-brown centres,
30cm (12in); *T. alata* 'Susie Black-Eyed Orange',
bright orange with black eye, 2m (6ft) when left to
climb. Flowering summer to early autumn

About the authors

Chris and Valerie Wheeler have many years' experience in raising and growing plants, both for their own garden and for the specialist nursery that they owned for over 15 years. They are keen plantsmen, having collected seeds – and plants – from many sources.

In addition to their writing and photography, they also run a mail-order business specializing in plant labelling.

As well as illustrating their books, Chris contributes pictures to photographic libraries and magazines, and has recently launched a range of greetings cards.

Chris and Valerie Wheeler have written four other books for GMC Publications Ltd – *Sink and Container Gardening Using Dwarf Hardy Plants; Gardening with Hebes, Alpine Gardening* and the companion to this book, *Success with Cuttings.*

Index

Pages highlighted in **bold** include illustrations of plants

Other books available from
GMC Publications Ltd

GARDENING

Alpine Gardening	Chris & Valerie Wheeler
Auriculas for Everyone: How to Grow and Show Perfect Plants	Mary Robinson
Beginners' Guide to Herb Gardening	Yvonne Cuthbertson
Beginners' Guide to Water Gardening	Graham Clarke
The Birdwatcher's Garden	Hazel & Pamela Johnson
Companions to Clematis: Growing Clematis with Other Plants	Marigold Badcock
Creating Contrast with Dark Plants	Freya Martin
Creating Small Habitats for Wildlife in your Garden	Josie Briggs
Exotics are Easy	GMC Publications
Gardening with Hebes	Chris & Valerie Wheeler
Gardening with Wild Plants	Julian Slatcher
Growing Cacti and Other Succulents in the Conservatory and Indoors	Shirley-Anne Bell
Growing Cacti and Other Succulents in the Garden	Shirley-Anne Bell
Growing Successful Orchids in the Greenhouse and Conservatory	Mark Isaac-Williams
Hardy Palms and Palm-Like Plants	Martyn Graham
Hardy Perennials: A Beginner's Guide	Eric Sawford
Hedges: Creating Screens and Edges	Averil Bedrich
Marginal Plants	Bernard Sleeman
Orchids are Easy: A Beginner's Guide to their Care and Cultivation	Tom Gilland
Plant Alert: A Garden Guide for Parents	Catherine Collins
Planting Plans for Your Garden	Jenny Shukman
Sink and Container Gardening Using Dwarf Hardy Plants	Chris & Valerie Wheeler
The Successful Conservatory and Growing Exotic Plants	Joan Phelan
Tropical Garden Style with Hardy Plants	Alan Hemsley
Water Garden Projects: From Groundwork to Planting	Roger Sweetinburgh

WOODCARVING

Beginning Woodcarving	GMC Publications
Carving Architectural Detail in Wood: The Classical Tradition	Frederick Wilbur
Carving Birds & Beasts	GMC Publications
Carving the Human Figure: Studies in Wood and Stone	Dick Onians
Carving Nature: Wildlife Studies in Wood	Frank Fox-Wilson
Carving on Turning	Chris Pye
Celtic Carved Lovespoons: 30 Patterns	Sharon Littley & Clive Griffin
Decorative Woodcarving (New Edition)	Jeremy Williams
Elements of Woodcarving	Chris Pye
Essential Woodcarving Techniques	Dick Onians
Lettercarving in Wood: A Practical Course	Chris Pye
Relief Carving in Wood: A Practical Introduction	Chris Pye
Woodcarving for Beginners	GMC Publications
Woodcarving Tools, Materials & Equipment (New Edition in 2 vols.)	Chris Pye

WOODTURNING

Bowl Turning Techniques Masterclass	Tony Boase
Chris Child's Projects for Woodturners	Chris Child
Contemporary Turned Wood: New Perspectives in a Rich Tradition	Ray Leier, Jan Peters & Kevin Wallace
Decorating Turned Wood: The Maker's Eye	Liz & Michael O'Donnell
Green Woodwork	Mike Abbott
Intermediate Woodturning Projects	GMC Publications
Keith Rowley's Woodturning Projects	Keith Rowley
Making Screw Threads in Wood	Fred Holder
Turned Boxes: 50 Designs	Chris Stott
Turning Green Wood	Michael O'Donnell
Turning Pens and Pencils	Kip Christensen & Rex Burningham
Woodturning: A Foundation Course (New Edition)	Keith Rowley
Woodturning: A Fresh Approach	Robert Chapman
Woodturning: An Individual Approach	Dave Regester
Woodturning: A Source Book of Shapes	John Hunnex
Woodturning Masterclass	Tony Boase
Woodturning Techniques	GMC Publications

MAGAZINES

WOODTURNING ● WOODCARVING ● FURNITURE & CABINETMAKING ● THE ROUTER
NEW WOODWORKING ● THE DOLLS' HOUSE MAGAZINE ● MACHINE KNITTING NEWS
● OUTDOOR PHOTOGRAPHY ● BLACK & WHITE PHOTOGRAPHY ● TRAVEL PHOTOGRAPHY
● GUILD OF MASTER CRAFTSMEN NEWS

The above represents a full list of all titles currently published or scheduled to be published.
All are available direct from the Publishers or through bookshops, newsagents and specialist retailers.

To place an order, or to obtain a complete catalogue, contact:

GMC Publications Ltd.,
Castle Place, 166 High Street, Lewes, East Sussex BN7 1XU, United Kingdom
Tel: 01273 488005 Fax: 01273 402866
E-mail: pubs@thegmcgroup.com
Orders by credit card are accepted